PERFECTING SOURDOUGH

First published in the UK in 2016 by
Apple Press
74–77 White Lion Street
London N1 9PF
United Kingdom
www.apple-press.com

QTT.PSOU

ISBN: 978-1-84543-650-6

Conceived, designed and produced by:
Quintet Publishing
4th Floor, Sheridan House
114–116 Western Road
Hove BN3 1DD
United Kingdom

Project Editor: Rachel Malig
Designer: Tania Gomes
Photographer: Jon Whitaker
Food Stylist: Lucy Heeley
Art Director: Michael Charles
Publisher: Mark Searle

10 9 8 7 6 5 4 3 2 1

Printed and bound in China by RR Donnelley

JANE MASON

PERFECTING SOURDOUGH

WITH ED WOOD *ET AL.*

APPLE

CONTENTS

FOREWORD

This is my third book about bread and I am delighted that it is a book on sourdough baking. I started experimenting with sourdough a long time ago when a friend gave me some of her wheat sourdough starter and a photocopy of an old American sourdough book that I still treasure. That wheat starter is now the stuff of legends, having been born in 1857, lived in many different countries, survived bus journeys and transatlantic flights, and lived through an accidental five-year exile to the back of the fridge. It is living proof of the hardiness of a sourdough culture.

Years later I bought some backferment from a health food shop in Germany and started experimenting with that, and then I got into baking with a rye starter. Along the way I have experimented with spelt, buckwheat and sprouted grain starters. Baking with sourdough is a life-long journey and every day is exciting, with a little frisson of danger! I would love to be able to tell you that every loaf has been a beauty but that would be a lie. There have been some spectacularly ugly loaves along the way but – repeat the mantra after me – everything is good toasted, even if it's ugly.

In this book we have included recipes for just two starters – rye and wheat – as you can achieve a great deal in the world of sourdough baking with just these two. It keeps things simple and you won't have numerous jars of starters cluttering up your fridge. If you like, you can make four starters because the process for making and using a light rye and a dark rye starter are the same, and the process for making a wholewheat starter and a white wheat starter are the same. This flexibility enables you to bake whole rye or wholewheat bread, or light rye or white wheat bread as your tastes dictate. If you get hooked (and beware, you may) you can go on experimenting forever with different grains, starters and doughs. There really is no end to what you can do.

Finally, it's worth mentioning that while baking sourdough bread might seem daunting – people frequently say that it takes forever – the reality is that it is actually simpler than baking other types of bread. That's because sourdough does its thing over so many hours that you're free to leave it and go to work or go to bed. Of course, all the recipes differ but there are plenty that will work around you and your schedule. The actual time you need to spend interacting with your dough is a matter of minutes, and once you make your starter you can keep it for life!

Jane Mason

INTRODUCTION

Over the past few years, sourdough baking has enjoyed a resurgence, as people discover that they actually like chewing their bread and enjoy the stronger flavour that sourdough offers. In addition, many people find they can eat and enjoy sourdough bread without feeling bloated and uncomfortable the way they sometimes do when they eat 'regular' bread.

BAKE YOUR OWN

Buying sourdough at a supermarket or market where you can't talk to the baker can be a bit of a risky business: there are no clear labelling laws for bread, and the dough of many 'sourdough' loaves is actually made with regular yeast with the addition of sourdough powders for flavour. That's where this book comes in – here you will find all the information you need, and a collection of recipes that are simple and clear, so you can have a go at making your own sourdough bread.

DEMYSTIFYING SOURDOUGH

Sourdough baking seems to have acquired a mystique, and one of the aims of this book is to demystify it. The truth is that baking sourdough bread is simple and intuitive – anyone can do it. One of the reasons sourdough baking seems so complicated is that there are many different words used in the world of sourdough baking – some mean the same thing and some don't – and different bakers use the same word to mean different things. Starter, poolish, biga, sponge, pre-dough, batter: the terms are often interchangeable and it can get a bit confusing. Don't worry – read on and we'll list the terms that are used throughout the book, and define them for you.

Another reason why baking sourdough bread seems complicated is that there are about a million ways to bake it. Again, don't worry – there is no one right way. Some bakers may go through stages that others do not, and some bread requires a particular process while other bread requires something quite different. The truth is that it all depends on what you are baking and how you choose to bake it.

This book aims to demystify the process of baking sourdough bread and to set out a simple, consistent process that will result in delicious and beautiful loaves time and time again. Of course, there are plenty of other books and many other ways in which to bake sourdough bread, and we encourage you to experiment and find the ways that work for you. We hope that this book helps you on your journey.

BREAD BASICS

IT'S ALL IN THE RISE

In order for dough to rise you need air bubbles to form in it, and you need the dough to have the strength to maintain those air bubbles and expand. So, the first thing you need is flour that will develop into dough that will puff out as the air bubbles form, rather than expand a bit and collapse.

Think of bubble gum. You can blow big bubbles with bubble gum because it was created especially to blow bubbles. However, 'regular' chewing gum only enables you to blow small bubbles before they pop. It is the same with flour: some grains make flour that creates a dough that is like bubble gum so, when air is inserted into it, it can support the formation of big bubbles. Other grains make flour that creates a dough that is like 'regular' chewing gum so, when air is inserted into it, it will only support the development of small bubbles before they collapse.

ADDING YEAST

The bubbles in bread are created when the yeast that is added to dough starts to eat the sugars in the flour, drink the water and burp. Seriously, when yeast begins to eat and drink, it emits carbon dioxide gas just like us. You can prepare your dough with yeast from a packet or with a sourdough starter, which is simply a paste of flour and water in which natural yeast has been trapped. Yeast is a micro-organism that lives in the air. There are yeasts in the air all around us and making a sourdough starter is a way of bottling them.

CHOOSING YOUR LOAF

The first things to decide before you start baking are what kind of bread you would like, how you are going to use it, and how much interaction you want with the dough as you prepare it for baking. These are important considerations because bread really does have a function and, like anything, there is a trade-off between time and effort, and results.

If you like the closed, dense structure of northern European-style bread – which you slice thinly and top with smoked fish, strong cheese or butter and jam – you may want to use a rye sourdough starter and bake bread with a high rye content. The benefit of this is that you will typically prepare the dough and put it straight into a tin or basket to rise before baking, so it requires almost no work at all. However, if you prefer French- or Italian-style bread, with a more open crumb that you tear to dip into sauce, or use to make sandwiches that the crust keeps together, you may want to use a wheat starter and bake with a high wheat content. To do this you will need to prepare your dough in two or three stages. Many people like their bread with big holes in the crumb. To achieve this, you need:

1. Wet dough that blisters easily as the bubbles are formed.
2. High protein flour to support the development of big bubbles.
3. Lots of stretching and folding to elongate the bubbles, thin the dough membranes and give the yeast fresh air and food to keep it working.
4. A very hot oven to ensure maximum 'oven spring' and rapid crust formation.

Extra proving for extra flavour

Many of the recipes in this book call for you to mix up the final dough, knead if required, shape it immediately and, when properly fermented, bake. However, if you would like to build the flavour of your dough and break down the flour more with a longer fermentation, you can do it.

Dough with a high rye content requires little or no kneading, but low or no rye-content dough benefits from kneading to activate the gluten and ensure a nice rise. If you would like to ferment the dough for longer than the recipes call for, you can do one of the following:

1. Mix all the ingredients together, cover the bowl and leave it for 2–3 hours before kneading. The flour will begin to ferment and the gluten becomes activated: this is called 'autolysing'. You could also put the bowl in the fridge overnight. Then, simply knead and shape the dough, following the recipe instructions for proving and baking.

2. You can knead half of the flour and water and pop the dough back in the bowl. Cover and leave the dough for 2–3 hours (or overnight in the fridge, if you like), then add the remaining ingredients and follow the recipe instructions for proving and baking. This will make the bread more chewy and it will have a stronger flavour.

If you have put the dough in the fridge, it will be cold, and will take several hours to come to room temperature and rise. You shouldn't leave your dough for much longer than outlined above. If your dough is too fermented it simply won't have any structure left to rise properly, and you will be left with very heavy loaves that may not brown nicely in the oven.

THE VERSATILE LOAF

The point is that there are many types of bread and many different styles of baking. For everyday bread, you may want something simple with only one or two steps, so you can get on with your life. But from time to time you may have the inclination to stay at home and fiddle with your dough at regular intervals to achieve a very different result. The important thing is to do what works for you.

Whether round or square, open or closed, baked in a tin or free form, made using rye or wheat (or anything else), the main, shared features of bread made with a sourdough starter – rather than packaged yeast – are the slightly acidic smell and taste, and the distinctive chewy texture. These characteristics are not for everyone – some people love them and some people don't.

SOURDOUGH BASICS

The process of baking with sourdough is similar to that of baking with fresh or dried yeast. There are, however, a few important differences:

1. It is very easy to make your own sourdough starter, but if you don't have a lab you can't make your own yeast – unless you already have some.

2. Sourdough starters can be stored indefinitely, as long as they are stored properly, whereas commercial yeast has a shelf life (unless you store it in the freezer).

3. The amount of sourdough starter you need to make bread is different to the amount of fresh or dried yeast you need to make bread. The amount of starter also depends on the base flour of the starter, the type of flour used to refresh the starter and the type of flour you use to make the final dough. Until you are familiar with your starters and how they behave when you refresh and bake with them, you can use recipes.

4. The sourdough starter must be refreshed (airy or bubbly, and sweet smelling) to make bread that rises. You can feed flour and water to your starter every day to keep it constantly refreshed. However, this is impractical for the home baker. It is far easier to store your starter in the fridge in an airtight container where it goes dormant. The day before you want to bake, take it out and refresh it. Every recipe in this book assumes your starter is stored in the fridge. It takes between 4 and 24 hours to refresh a dormant sourdough starter, depending on how long it has been sleeping. You will know the starter is refreshed when it is lively, bubbly and sweet smelling. You can test it by gently dribbling a teaspoon of starter into a glass of water: if it floats, it is good to use, if it sinks, it is not. If your starter sinks, just leave it for a little while longer and it will perk up.

5. Sourdough bread takes longer to rise. You can make good bread at home with commercial yeast in about 4 hours (minimum and on a hot day), but sourdough bread can take much longer. Don't panic, as most of that time is spent with the dough sitting around contemplating itself, and it does not require your attention.

6. It is this enforced longer fermentation (the time the dough is sitting around in its various stages before you bake it) that makes sourdough bread easier to digest than bread made in a shorter time. Over the hours, the yeast is actually eating

Storing your sourdough starter: Three Options

1. Put it in an airtight container and store in the fridge.
2. Weigh it and smear it on greaseproof paper, then let it dry completely. Weigh it again, crumble it and pop it in an airtight container. Store on a shelf in a cupboard and write the difference between the 'wet weight' and 'dry weight' on the container. That is the amount of water you need to add to reconstitute it before you refresh it according to the recipe.
3. Put it in an airtight container and freeze it (defrost before you use it).

the flour and breaking it down so we can digest it efficiently, and quickly extract the nutrients. This means that it doesn't hang around fermenting in our digestive systems, making us feel bloated.

7. Sourdough bread doesn't rise as much as bread made with commercial yeast (which is more powerful). With commercial yeast the dough should at least double in size at whatever stage, whereas sourdough bread will only rise by about one-and-a-half times before the yeast begins to lose its puff. The relative weakness of the natural yeast in a sourdough starter is one reason why the dough should be wetter than you may be used to. All else being equal, wetter dough expands more easily than drier dough.

Dough with a very high rye content is ready to bake when you start seeing holes in the surface of the dough. Because rye's gluten is weaker than wheat's, the air bubbles will eventually burst through the surface of the dough. Dough with a high wheat content is ready to bake when it passes the 'probe test'. Poke the loaf gently with your finger, making a little indentation. If the dough springs back and the indentation disappears in under a minute, it is ready to bake. If the dough is firm and the indentation stays, it is not ready.

If you put the dough in the oven at this stage, it may split because the dough is not sufficiently relaxed to withstand the 'oven spring' without splitting. It will be a little dense but it will still taste good. On the other hand, if the dough is very soft and airy and your finger goes straight through, you have let it over rise. In this instance, pull the dough out of the tin or basket, give it some more flour, knead gently, reshape, put it back in the container and let it rise again. Chalk it up to experience and have fun trying again.

8. Sourdough bread may taste a little stronger and have a chewier texture than bread made with commercial yeast. Sourdough bread doesn't need to taste sour: the longer you take to put your final dough together, and the more 'sour' you have as a proportion of new flour, the more acidic it will smell and taste. If you like a more acidic taste, select the recipes that take a lot of time to make and have more 'sour'. If you prefer a less acidic taste, choose recipes that take less time and have less 'sour'. As you develop your baking skills you will be able to adjust any recipe to suit your tastes. The term 'sourdough' is therefore a little misleading, and many bakers refer to sourdough bread as wild yeast bread or natural yeast bread instead.

MAKING YOUR OWN STARTERS

It is simple to make your own starters and there are many ways in which to do it. Some recipes ask you to use a little yeast, and some ask for a little grape, apple, vinegar or pineapple. I have even heard of one that asks for beer. Some recipes ask you to throw away some of your starter every day while you are making it. You can experiment to your heart's content or you can follow the recipes in this book which call only for flour and water.

In the book we use two different starters: rye (see page 40 for rye starter recipe) and wheat (see page 71 for wheat starter recipe). They behave differently and you may as well make one of each so you can bake your way through the book and decide which one you like better or whether you like both. You can make starters out of many other grains (any other grain, if I am being honest) but we only have space for two.

BASIC TERMS

A shared vocabulary is always a good thing so that everyone understands everyone else. Below are the terms that you will find used throughout the book, so you'll know exactly what we're referring to.

Sourdough starter

For the purposes of this book, the sourdough starter is the smelly gloop in the fridge that you need to wake up (refresh) before you put your dough together. Don't worry if your sourdough starter is really smelly, and don't worry if it has separated so there is liquid floating on the top of a mass of sediment – that's normal. The liquid is called hooch and you can ferment other things with this (like cabbage to make sauerkraut or fruit to make alcohol, but that's a whole other book). There's also no need to worry if the liquid is a dark brown colour. The time to start worrying is if your starter is mouldy, and if this is the case, throw it away. As long as you store your starter correctly (in an airtight container in the fridge, in the freezer or dehydrated) it will be just fine.

Refreshed starter

For the purposes of this book, the refreshed starter is the sweet-smelling result of adding flour and water to the possibly smelly sourdough starter from the fridge. How you refresh your starter varies according to the type of starter you are refreshing, and the type of bread you are making. Don't worry, the instructions are in every single recipe.

Pre-dough (not always necessary)

When there is an intermediate step (or steps) between refreshing the sourdough starter and kneading and shaping the final dough, this mixing together of ingredients is called making a pre-dough. Not all recipes call for a pre-dough, but you can make one if you want to, in order to strengthen the flavour of your bread.

Final dough

The final mixture that is eventually shaped and baked.

Your first sourdough bread

- Start by preparing a starter following the method on page 40 for a rye starter, and on page 71 for a wheat starter.
- Take a look at the equipment list on pages 18–20.
- Read through the advice on pages 26–27 on Storing and Using a Sourdough Starter.
- If you are new to baking with sourdough, you may like to begin by making the Finnish Rye (page 46) or the Mixed Grain Sourdough (page 78); both are pretty straight forward.
- Once you have mastered some of the basic recipes, have a go at different techniques – try Pitta Bread (page 81) or Cinnamon Rolls (page 130).

INGREDIENTS

YEAST

Commercial yeast that we can see and hold in our hands was invented in the 1850s but was not widely used until after the Second World War. We have been baking leavened bread for at least 10,000 years, using sourdough all the while.

We have already talked about the fact that the yeast we add to sourdough bread does not come from a packet: we can't see it or hold it. The yeast we add to sourdough bread is, in fact, trapped in the paste of flour and water that we call the sourdough starter. So, the starter contains the yeast.

Because you need to account for the weight of the flour and water that make the paste in which the yeast is trapped, and for the fact that natural yeast is weaker than commercial yeast, you need relatively more starter than yeast from a packet to make the same amount of bread. Also, because you are adding starter (with the consistency of sticky paste) rather than yeast (with the consistency of a powder or crumbly paste) to flour and water to make the dough, your sourdough bread dough will always be sticky. Sticky is normal; sticky is good.

FLOUR

From field to field, season to season, mill to mill and bag to bag, flour changes. It absorbs more or less water, is more or less stretchy, has more or less flavour, and has different colour variations. Bakers need to adjust to those changes, for example, by adding more or less water to the dough, letting the dough rise for more or less time, or expecting a higher or a lower rise.

Time and experience will teach you how to adjust, and you will constantly be adjusting as the seasons turn, as you change the brand (or even bag) of flour you use, and as the conditions in the kitchen change.

No bread recipe is a science and you will learn which texture of dough leads you to bake the bread you love. You will not bake these recipes with the same flour I used to test them so you may need to make adjustments: a little more or less water; a little more or less time. Never give up – your loaves may not be beauties all the time (I still get ugly ducklings) but as we've already learnt, everything is good toasted.

Wheat flour

Wheat flour is easily available in most countries around the world. It comes in different strengths and levels of fineness and whiteness. Unfortunately, there is no universal system for labelling flour so, if you move around, you may need to ask professional bakers what the names or numbers on the bag of flour mean. I have used 11 per cent gluten wheat flour to test the recipes. This is considered strong bread flour. If you can get that, great. If not, use what you can get.

Einkorn, emmer, spelt and kamut flour

All these flours are milled from grains that are distant cousins of wheat. They all have stretchy gluten and perform in a similar way to wheat flour. However, depending on how and where they are grown, they may be more or less strong and stretchy, or more or less absorbent than the wheat flour you are used to. The spelt I have used is as strong and as absorbent as the wheat. However, that is not always the case.

You can use these flours as substitutes for wheat flour, but every time you change grain you will notice a change in the amount of liquid the flour will absorb (you can modify the recipe by adding more or less liquid). The texture of the dough will also change (it may be more or less stretchy and expand more or less than when using wheat flour) and, of course, the appearance, texture and flavour of the final bread will be different. Again, time and experience will help you make those changes with ease, confidence and style.

Rye flour

Rye has gluten but it is not stretchy like the gluten in the wheat family, so it doesn't handle or perform in the same way. You can't substitute wheat for rye or rye for wheat. Also, rye is much more absorbent than wheat so expect it to absorb a lot more liquid. Your rye dough should always be wet – anything less than wet leads to the leaden loaves that people understandably don't appreciate very much. If you bake one of these, put it down to experience. Add more liquid next time and, in the meantime, slice your leaden rye very, very thinly and toast it. Remember the mantra? That's right – everything is good toasted.

Non-glutinous flour

There are more non-glutinous grains than glutinous grains. Millet, barley, rice, quinoa and buckwheat are all examples of non-glutinous grains that are milled into flour. They are not substitutes for grains with gluten – they can make lovely bread but you need to treat them in a specialised way to do so. This book does not include gluten-free recipes.

Sprouted flour

Sprouted flour is becoming very popular and it's fun to work with. In general, you can substitute sprouted flour for non-sprouted flour. However, the dough will feel and perform differently and the final bread will look very different too. When you buy sprouted grains, there are usually instructions on the packet to advise you how to use it and what to expect. There are no sprouted grain recipes in this book.

WATER

Use water straight from your cold tap, or filtered water at room temperature. Sourdough bread does not need warm water, and the only thing that will kill yeast is heat. So don't second-guess or stress about your water temperature – just use ordinary water.

SALT

Bread needs salt for flavour so please use it. Salt slows down yeast activity and some bakers add it partway through the kneading process. If you find you tend to forget to add the salt when you're kneading, add it at the beginning; it won't make much difference to the final product.

EQUIPMENT

KILNER JAR OR CLIPPED TUPPERWARE

Store your starter in a Kilner jar or a plastic container with clip-down sides. A jam jar is risky, as your starter will continue to ferment and thus let off carbon dioxide gas as it goes to sleep in your fridge. Jam jars don't have a mechanism for allowing gas to leave them and there's a possibility that the jar will shatter. Kilner jars, on the other hand, let air out without letting air in, and plastic containers are fine as long as they are properly airtight and all sides snap down. Plastic containers that just have a snap-on lid are not sufficiently airtight and you risk killing your starter by using them.

BAKING TINS

Baking tins are great for many reasons:
- You can clearly see how the dough is moving – has it risen and by how much?
- Your loaves will look perfect every time with no unseemly bulges that accompany a poorly shaped loaf that you have proved in a basket.
- When you grease a tin properly (with hard fat like butter or lard) the bread will come out of the tin every time. With baskets there is always a little uncertainty – will it or won't it stick?

PROVING BASKETS (BANNETONS)

Proving baskets (see photograph above) are made of cane or pressed fibres, and they hold the dough during its final rise. We learnt to work with cane long before we learnt to work with metal so they have been used to shape bread for hundreds, if not thousands, of years. Proving baskets give the baked loaf an attractive finish (with rings of flour on top of the loaves). You can buy them from cooking or baking stores, and from specialist websites.

Before using the proving basket, season it by painting a thin mixture of cornflour and water all over the basket with a small paintbrush and leave it to dry. When proving sourdough loaves in baskets, liberally flour both basket and dough to make sure it doesn't stick. Place the shaped dough in the basket top side down. This is because you invert the dough out of the basket and onto a baking sheet so it is sitting right side up to bake it. You don't put proving baskets in the oven. After a few uses, scrub the basket with hot, soapy water and let it dry completely before you use it again. They do need washing from time to time. Remember to season the basket after washing.

Today, you can buy proving baskets made of plastic as well as cane. They work well, the bread looks authentic and they can go in the dishwasher.

OTHER CONTAINERS

Ceramic or glass bowls, strainers, flower pots, saucepans, frying pans… I have probably tried them all, given that I have been in plenty of places which have neither tins nor proving baskets. If the container is ovenproof and you want to bake your bread in it, make sure you grease it well with a hard fat before putting the dough inside. If the container isn't ovenproof, line it with a tea towel that you have floured liberally before gently laying your shaped, floured dough in it. As with shaping in a proving basket, place your shaped dough in the container upside down, as you will turn it out of the container onto a baking sheet to bake it.

COUCHE (BAKING CLOTH)

Baking is very tea towel intensive. No matter how many you have, you always seem to need more. Certain types of bread (notably baguettes and ciabattas) are proved on cloths, and heavy linen cloths made specifically for proving are now readily available from baking stores or dedicated websites. Flour the cloth and the dough well to ensure it doesn't stick and put the dough on upside down to prove. When the dough is ready, pick it up, turn it over and lay it on the baking sheet. You don't have to do this, but it gives the bread a nice floury look and it ensures the air bubbles are evenly distributed.

BAKING SHEETS

If you prove your bread in, or on, anything other than a tin you will need some good baking sheets. It is worth paying a little extra for sturdy sheets that do not warp in the oven. Even if your sheet states it is non-stick, it pays to line the sheet when you bake bread – you can use polenta, semolina or non-stick baking parchment. If using polenta or semolina, simply scatter some liberally on the baking sheet and place the dough on top – it acts as a barrier between the dough and the sheet. If you're using baking parchment make sure it is clearly labelled as non-stick. Tear a piece from the roll, fold or cut it to fit your sheet, and place the dough directly on the paper. You can reuse baking parchment until it falls apart.

LAME

A lame is a straight-edged razor on a stick that bakers use to make the cuts in their loaves. A thin, sharp blade handled with confidence will make a beautiful pattern on your crust and help control any cracking that may occur as your loaves are baking. There are dozens of videos on the internet about how to use a lame to best advantage, but be warned – it's not as easy as it looks. Your first few attempts will leave you with what look like healed scars on your bread, but persevere, as it will get easier and your cuts will get better. Lames are readily available on specialist baking websites.

BOWLS

You will need some big bowls to refresh the sourdough starter and to build your dough. It's a good idea to have a few in the cupboard for when you want to make more than one loaf.

PLASTIC SCRAPERS

Plastic scrapers will change your life. Sourdough dough is sticky, and scrapers help you knead, shape, cut and move the dough around without leaving half of it either on your hands or on the surface. They also help you clean up more easily by enabling you to scrape down your counter.

PLASTIC SHOWER CAPS

Sourdough bread takes time to rise, so covering the dough with a tea towel can result in the dough drying out. Also, as the dough is sticky, a tea towel or cling film may pull the top surface of the dough off as you pull them away from the dough. Shower caps, on the other hand, are pretty airtight because they are elasticated, and because they are puckered and pleated, you can fit them around the edge of a tin or bowl and puff them up to give the dough plenty of headroom to rise without sticking to anything. You don't need anything fancy – you can use the kind that you find in hotels – and you can buy them in bulk (they're not expensive) from hotel supply companies or from Amazon or other online stores.

DIGITAL SCALES AND MEASURING SPOONS

Although sourdough baking is not a precise science, there are some ratios you need to respect in order to get good results. The ratio of sourdough starter to water to flour is one that's important, and the ratio of refreshed starter to water to flour is another. Beginners should measure as accurately as possible, but with just a little experience you'll find you can bake by feeling. To that end, most ingredients in this book are listed in grams – even the liquids. Invest in a little digital scale and you will see a big difference in the results of your bread making.

BAKING STONE

In some countries bread is baked by sliding the dough directly onto the floor of the oven, and you can mimic this environment by buying a baking stone and popping the dough straight onto that to bake. If you want to use this method, you will also need to buy a peel. This is a long-handled instrument with a 'paddle' on the end – you may have seen them used in pizza restaurants. Stones and peels are expensive but many people use them at home and swear by them, so it could be a good investment.

A cheaper alternative is to buy a couple of good-quality metal baking sheets. Place the sheets in the oven to heat while the oven is heating. When you are ready to bake, remove the sheets and line them with non-stick baking parchment (remember it's hot) or sprinkle with a layer of polenta or semolina. Place the dough on top and then pop the sheets in the oven.

OVEN

Sourdough dough loves heat, and, for some recipes, the higher your oven can go, the better the result. A new oven is expensive, but an oven thermometer to test if your oven reaches the correct temperature is not. If your oven is way out, get an engineer to calibrate it. A good-quality electric oven is best for bread, as it can reach a high temperature and the heat is evenly distributed. Gas ovens tend to have uneven heat distribution, and fan ovens that circulate hot air around can dry out the surface of the bread.

MIXER

Stand mixers help when kneading but I recommend you begin kneading by hand to become accustomed to the texture of the dough. If you don't touch the dough you can't test the texture or compare textures between one recipe and another, and one grain and another. There is no 'right' texture – different recipes will have different textures and it's important to learn that. Once you get to know the texture you want to achieve, you can knead in a machine and test for texture by giving the dough a little squeeze to see if it is soft or wet enough. Knowing how different textures of dough perform is a matter of experience, and over time you will become more confident and be able to adjust mid-knead in order to achieve the desired results. The recipes in this book ask you to knead the dough for 10 minutes. Whether kneading by hand or machine, aim for 10 minutes. The exception is pure rye which requires no kneading. If you are using a machine, you may need to stop it several times to turn the dough over by hand while it is kneading. This is because the average machine is not designed to manage heavier dough. They tend to leave a lot of flour at the bottom of the bowl.

PLANT MISTER

A plant mister is useful for misting the top of a loaf in order to 'stick' ingredients like seeds onto it. It can also be useful for spraying the inside of the oven to increase humidity for certain bakes.

Equipment essentials

If you are new to bread making or simply don't fancy forking out on specialist equipment, the following items will enable you to get started:

- Kilner jar or clipped tupperware
- Baking tins in your chosen sizes
- Baking sheet
- Bowls
- A digital scale
- Measuring spoons
- Oven thermometer
- Digital probe thermometer

BATTER BREAD

Batter breads are fun and just a little bit different from an ordinary pancake, muffin or tea cake. The sourdough starter adds flavour, changes texture and, in some recipes, acts as a fat replacement. These recipes are a great place to start when you are baking with children as there is a little less time to wait before sampling the finished product.

BATTER BAKING BASICS

Batter is a curious word. It refers to an almost liquid mixture of flour with other ingredients, and we usually think of pancakes, waffles or Yorkshire puddings when talking about recipes made with batter. However, there are so many more kinds of bread you can make with batter, and they are really easy to prepare, as they don't require kneading.

PANCAKES AND WAFFLES

Of course pancakes and waffles do not require yeast – natural or otherwise. Typically, they are made with bicarbonate of soda or baking powder, both of which act as the raising agent. However, pancakes and waffles made with sourdough are worth trying for a few reasons, and they don't require much more work than regular pancakes or waffles: they just take a bit of advanced planning. As the flour lies around doing its thing, it develops flavour, and the many hours it spends fermenting makes the resulting pancakes and waffles really easy to digest.

BATTER BREAD

To make batter bread, you simply spoon the batter into a tin and bake it. The resulting bread is similar to a 'quick bread' or a 'tea loaf'. The loaves are moist and flavourful with a dense crumb that is more like a muffin than a loaf of bread. Batter breads make a wonderful alternative to 'regular' bread and, as with the waffles and pancakes, the flavour is deliciously strong, and the bread is easy to digest.

BASIC SOURDOUGH BATTER BREAD

Makes about 600 ml batter

INGREDIENTS

65 g wheat sourdough starter (page 71)
345 g white wheat or spelt flour
65 g water
100 g melted butter or vegetable oil, plus
  extra for greasing

100 g sugar
120 g milk
1 egg
¾ tsp baking powder
jam and butter, to serve

METHOD

Day one

1. Measure the sourdough starter into a large bowl and return any remaining starter to the fridge.
2. Add 65 g flour and all the water. Stir and cover with cling film, and leave on the counter for around 8 hours.

Day two

3. In a large mixing bowl, mix the butter or oil, sugar, milk and egg together. Sift in the remaining flour and baking powder and then add the refreshed starter. Stir to eliminate any lumps but don't over mix. The batter is thick, but if it's too thick you can slacken it with a drop of milk.
4. Scrape the batter into a 20 x 20 cm greased baking tin.
5. Cover with a shower cap and leave to rest for 3 hours.
6. Preheat the oven to 200°C. Place the tin in the oven and bake for 40 minutes.
7. Remove the loaf from the tin and leave to cool on a wire rack.
8. Serve with generous quantities of jam and butter.

Batter Bread

STORING AND USING A SOURDOUGH STARTER

Once you have made your starter, you can use some immediately, but don't use it all or you will need to make another batch before you bake again. It's important to hold some back for the next time you want to bake. In order to keep your starter and pass it down to your grandchildren, you need to care for it properly, and to do this you have two options.

OPTION 1: Keep your starter in a permanent state of refreshment

Realistically, if you are not baking in volume, this option is not really viable. You probably won't use enough starter to keep a manageable vat that stays lively. However, if you really want to feed the starter every day, give it a try. Just add enough flour and water to your starter to maintain its consistency. You may find that one of these things happens:

- The amount of starter you have grows because you're not using it.
- The starter gets weaker as it gets older. This is because you have an increasingly large amount of starter to which you are adding a relatively small amount of new food. The yeast eats the new food in record time (you will see it froth almost instantly, then, an hour later, it's calm again) and goes to sleep. Sleepy yeast does not make great bread, which is why some methods tell you to throw half your starter away on a regular basis. I'm against this method because I don't believe in wasting food.
- You forget about your starter and it dies.

Professional bakers use lots of starter and they put lots of flour and water back every day. Nevertheless, many of them put their starters in the fridge every night just in case.

OPTION 2: Refresh your starter when you need it

You can freeze your starter, you can dry your starter, you can refrigerate it in an airtight container, and it will just go to sleep. That way, you can ignore it until the next time you want to bake. What you can't do is leave it in a liquid state at room temperature much longer than a couple of days without feeding it. At room temperature the yeast will eventually eat everything in sight and then starve to death. At that point, the starter will go mouldy and die. If your starter has mould on it, it is best to throw it away. I once found some starter in the back of the fridge that had been there for about five years. I refreshed it (which took two days), and it was as good as new.

To refresh the starter when you need it, simply follow the instructions in the recipe. The recipes in this book assume you will store your starter in the fridge and that it will need refreshing. To that end, they build in refreshment time, and you get used to planning this in advance. In five minutes you have taken out your starter and fed it, and then you can go to bed or go to work and pick up the process later.

The recipes ask you to measure the amount of starter you need into a bowl and put the rest back into the fridge. When you see the amount of starter in the fridge is getting low, you just top it up. The instructions for making starters tell you how to top them up. The process for rye and wheat is different.

If you kill your starter, it's not the end of the world, as you can make more in four days. It is not the same as running out of yeast – when that happens you have to find a shop and buy more.

STORING BREAD

Many kinds of sourdough bread (especially those with a high rye content) are very 'damp' when they come out of the oven. You should wait until your bread is completely cool before cutting into it because the final structure of the crumb is still forming as the bread cools. You can certainly wait 24–48 hours before cutting into the bread and it will still be fantastic. After the bread is cool, and while you wait, simply wrap the loaf in a tea towel and leave it on the counter. Or pop it in a metal or ceramic bread bin.

Makes 20 pancakes of about 10 cm in diameter

YUKON FLAPJACKS

- -

Make sure the pan is very hot before pouring on the batter. When bubbles start to appear and the edges go brown, it is time to turn the flapjacks over.

INGREDIENTS

85 g wheat sourdough starter (page 71)
225 g white wheat or spelt flour (whole or white)
85 g water
120 g milk (or water or milk substitute)
½ tsp salt
1 tsp baking powder
50 g sugar
2 tbsp melted butter, lard or vegetable oil, plus extra for greasing
2 eggs
jam or maple syrup, to serve

METHOD

Day one

1. Measure the sourdough starter into a large bowl and return any remaining starter to the fridge.
2. Add 85 g flour (of your choice) and all the water. Stir and cover with cling film, and leave on the counter for around 8 hours.

Day two

3. Add all of the remaining ingredients to the refreshed starter and whisk well to get rid of any lumps. Heat a large, heavy frying pan to medium–high heat and add a little butter or oil to grease the pan. Use a large spoon or jug to pour the batter into the pan, forming rounds.
4. Cook for 3–4 minutes, until bubbles form over the top of the pancakes and the edges are golden.
5. Flip the pancakes and cook on the other side for 2–3 minutes. Serve hot with jam or maple syrup.

Batter Bread

Makes a 950 g loaf

BATTER BREAD WITH CRANBERRY AND BLUEBERRY

- -

Cranberries have become an increasingly popular ingredient in baking, and when partnered with fresh blueberries, the combination is hard to beat.

INGREDIENTS

65 g wheat sourdough starter (page 71)

345 g white wheat or spelt flour

65 g water

100 g melted butter or vegetable oil, plus extra for greasing

100 g sugar

120 g milk

1 egg

¾ tsp baking powder

75 g cranberries

75 g blueberries

flaked almonds, to cover

TIP:

You can add just about anything you fancy to batter bread – consider it an alternative to a tea cake or a fruit loaf. Options include:

- 1 apple, peeled and chopped into small pieces; or a little apple purée and 1 tsp cinnamon
- 1 chopped banana
- a handful of raisins, chopped apricots, dates or candied ginger
- a handful of raspberries
- a handful of chopped walnuts, pecans, almonds or hazelnuts
- a handful of chocolate chips

Do not omit the almonds (unless you are allergic to nuts). This loaf does not really brown and is a bit plain when it comes out of the oven unless you decorate it with something that will take on colour.

METHOD

Day one

1. Measure the sourdough starter into a large bowl and return any remaining starter to the fridge.
2. Add 65 g flour and all the water. Stir and cover with cling film, and leave on the counter for around 8 hours.

Day two

3. In a large mixing bowl, mix the butter or oil, sugar, milk and egg together. Sift in the remaining flour and baking powder and then add the refreshed starter. Stir to eliminate any lumps but don't over mix. The batter is thick, but if it's too thick you can slacken it with a drop of milk.
4. Add the fruit and fold in gently to distribute it evenly.
5. Scrape the batter into a 20 x 20 cm greased baking tin. Scatter a handful of almonds over the top.
6. Cover with a shower cap and leave to rest for 3 hours.
7. Preheat the oven to 200°C. Place the tin in the oven and bake for 40 minutes. Check after 20 minutes, and if the almonds are getting too brown, cover the top with some greaseproof paper or foil.
8. Remove the loaf from the tin and leave to cool on a wire rack.

FLUFFY WAFFLES

As the name suggests, this recipe results in light, fluffy waffles that are perfect for breakfast.
Serve with fresh fruit and maple syrup.

INGREDIENTS

260 g wheat sourdough starter (page 71)
200 g white wheat or spelt flour
60 g water
240 g milk
50 g sugar
2 tbsp melted butter, lard or vegetable oil
4 eggs, separated
¼ tsp salt
1 tsp baking powder
fresh fruit and maple syrup, to serve

METHOD

Day one

1. Measure the sourdough starter into a large bowl and return any remaining starter to the fridge.
2. Add 100 g flour and all the water. Stir and cover with cling film, and leave on the counter for around 8 hours.

Day two

3. Add the remaining flour, the milk, sugar, butter or oil, egg yolks, salt and baking powder to the refreshed starter and stir well to remove any lumps.
4. In a separate bowl, beat the egg whites to soft peaks.
5. Add the beaten egg whites to the main mixture and fold them in gently.
4. Heat an electric waffle iron and follow the instructions for making perfect waffles.
5. Serve hot with fresh fruit and maple syrup.

 TIP:
You can use this batter to make pancakes if you do not have a waffle iron.

SOUR CREAM WAFFLES

The addition of sour cream gives these waffles a rich flavour and fluffy texture. Serve with extra sour cream and sweet fruit compote.

INGREDIENTS

260 g wheat sourdough starter (page 71)
140 g white wheat or spelt flour
100 g water
150 g sour cream, buttermilk or full-fat natural yoghurt
1 tbsp melted butter, lard or vegetable oil
½ tsp baking powder
50 g sugar
1 egg, separated
pinch of salt
sour cream and fruit compote, to serve

METHOD

Day one

1. Measure the sourdough starter into a large bowl and return any remaining starter to the fridge.
2. Add 70 g flour and all the water. Stir and cover with cling film, and leave on the counter for around 8 hours.

Day two

3. Add the remaining flour, the sour cream, butter or oil, sugar, egg yolk, salt and baking powder to the refreshed starter and stir well to remove any lumps.
4. In a separate bowl, beat the egg white to soft peaks.
5. Add the beaten egg white to the main mixture and fold in gently. Your batter should have the consistency of single cream; if it is too thick, add a little milk or water.
6. Heat an electric waffle iron and follow the instructions for making perfect waffles.
7. Serve hot with sour cream and fruit compote.

EVERYDAY RYE

Begin by making a rye starter (page 40) and you can immediately try your hand at Pure Rye bread (page 45), which has the added benefit of requiring no kneading. A great first recipe.

RYE BAKING BASICS

Rye is the staple bread in most of northern Europe and Russia, for the simple reason that rye is the grain that traditionally grew in these regions. Wheat is a relatively recent crop, and while it is popular for bread baking, rye remains the dominant grain.

Rye flour has a wonderful flavour, is easy to work with, and rye bread is delicious when paired with traditional northern European foods (strong cheese, smoked, pickled and fermented fish, meat and vegetables). Rye contains gluten but it is a different type of gluten than that found in wheat and the wheat family. The gluten in rye isn't stretchy, which means a couple of things:

1. You can't shape rye dough the way you shape dough made with wheat flour: it just breaks if you pull on it.
2. It will never rise as high as dough made with wheat flour because the carbon dioxide bubbles that develop when the yeast gets to work eventually burst through the surface of the rye dough, as the fragile gluten breaks.
3. Your loaf will never have the high dome of bread made with wheat flour. Rye loaves are normally flatter than wheat loaves.
4. Your loaf will always be denser, with smaller bubbles, in a more closed crumb structure. However, the dense structure doesn't result in heavy, brick-like bread – if it does, your dough was probably too dry. Rye absorbs a lot of water and the dough should be soft and feel smooth. If the dough is dry and/or gritty, gradually add more water until it is soft and smooth.

KNEADING RYE DOUGH

Kneading dough with rye flour can be a challenge if you're not used to it. It has a texture that is both sticky and slimy. If you are making 100 per cent rye bread you don't actually need to knead it at all. If you

are mixing rye and wheat, however, the results will be better if you knead the dough in order to activate the stretchy gluten in the wheat flour.

Be prepared to get messy – you will find it easier if you use a scraper. Push the dough away from you with the heel of your hand and gather it back into a pile with the scraper. Repeat, repeat, repeat, adding more water, as necessary, if the dough becomes too hard and dry. If you are using a machine, use the paddle attachment and turn the dough over by hand several times while kneading.

SHAPING RYE DOUGH

Shaping rye dough requires wet hands. Dough sticks to dough so, when you are ready to shape your dough, have a bowl of water beside you.

Gather the dough together in a ball in the bowl or on the counter with a scraper. Then, with very wet hands, scoop it up and pass it from hand to hand. Hold it in the right hand and smooth the surface with the left hand, then transfer it to the left hand and smooth the surface with the right hand. Try to keep the shape to the same size as the container and continue to smooth it until it is like a small brick or ball, depending on the recipe. When it is the right shape, gently place it in the container and flour generously if the recipe asks you to. Don't squash it to fit – the dough will rise and fill the corners.

BAKING RYE BREAD

Rye does not necessarily sound hollow when it is baked – sometimes it's just a bit too dense for that. However, the bottom crust will feel thin when

you tap it, a bit like tapping an empty Tupperware container. If you're concerned you won't get it right, buy a probe thermometer. The inside temperature of bread when it is baked is 98°C.

Finally, because dough made with rye flour must be highly hydrated in order for the bread to be light, the bread is often damp. This is a double-edged sword: on the one hand, you really don't want to cut into rye bread until it is at least 24 hours old, which means you have to wait. On the other hand, it will be delicious, moist and edible for 5–6 days – it really does stay fresh for ages. To store it, wrap it in a tea towel and put it in a bread bin made of tin, ceramic or glass. That way it won't go mouldy quickly either.

✥ FAST FACT: SLOWLY DOES IT

Many people believe sourdough bread to be healthier than other types of bread. However, it is not that sourdough bread is necessarily better for you – any long-fermentation bread is better than bread that is fermented over a short time.

Bread rises because the yeast eats the flour and breaks it down in a particular chemical process called fermentation. This process creates the gas that makes the dough rise. When bread dough goes through a long fermentation process, the flour is broken down more than during a short fermentation. So, the longer the bread takes to ferment, the easier it is to digest. Sourdough takes ages to ferment.

MAKING A RYE SOURDOUGH STARTER

Day one

Mix 50 g whole rye flour and 100 g water together in a large bowl. Cover with cling film or place a dinner plate over the bowl, and put it on the counter for 24 hours.

Day two

Add 50 g whole rye flour and 100 g water to the mix in the bowl. Stir, cover it, and put it on the counter for 24 hours.

Day three

Add 50 g whole rye flour and 100 g water to the mix in the bowl. Stir, cover it, and put it on the counter for 24 hours.

Day four

Add 50 g whole rye flour and 100 g water to the mix in the bowl. Stir, cover it, and put it on the counter for 24 hours.

Day five

Your starter should be bubbly – if it is, you have a viable starter. If not, don't add any more flour or water, just cover it and let it sit for another 24 hours. However, if nothing has happened by day six, it could be that your house is just too clean, or the air where you live is polluted and sadly lacking in natural yeast (unusual, but it happens). You could stop using bleach or antiseptic sprays on your kitchen surfaces, and revert to hot, soapy water for cleaning, and try again.

Your starter should be bubbly and lively: if it is, you're ready to start making sourdough bread, if not, put it down to experience and try again.

Day two

Day four

Day five

READY TO BAKE

You now have plenty of starter to use straight away in any recipe that calls for a rye starter. You also have plenty to put back into a container in the fridge to take out when you need it. When you put it back in the fridge use a large container, as your starter will continue to froth up before it calms down. If your container is too small, you might find starter all over the fridge the following morning. After a day or two it will calm down, go quiet and separate into the liquid that floats on top and the sediment that settles on the bottom.

THE GOLDEN RULE: DON'T RUN OUT OF SOURDOUGH STARTER

If you run out, you will have to make another, or find a friend who has one. You can do one of two things:

1. When you are following a 100 per cent rye recipe, you can refresh twice as much sourdough starter as the recipe calls for, and put what you don't need back in the container in the fridge.

2. When you get down to a small amount of sourdough starter in the fridge (50 g or so), simply top up the container. The refreshment ratio is 1:3:6. Weigh the starter and place it in a big bowl. Add three times as much rye flour and six times as much water as starter. Stir, cover, and leave for 8 hours or so. Your vat of rye sourdough starter is topped up.

PROBLEM

Your bread is cracked along the side. The crack may be along the top of a loaf that you have baked in a tin, or along the bottom of a loaf that you have baked on a baking tray.

SOLUTION

You have not proved the dough for long enough before putting it in the oven.

Dough springs up when it hits the heat of the oven and if your dough is not sufficiently relaxed it will crack rather than stretch. A high content rye (80 per cent or more) will develop little holes in the top when it is ready for the oven. Any other dough should pass the 'probe' test (page 13).

PROBLEM

Your bread has exploded out of the tin. It may develop a crack in the middle of the loaf on the top and explode out of that, or it will develop a crack along the side that completely separates the top of the loaf from its body.

SOLUTION

You have too much dough in your tin.

If you are baking 100 per cent rye, you can get away with filling your tin about five-sixths full. If you are baking just about anything else, limit the amount of dough to two-thirds of the tin. You may get a stumpy little loaf but at least it will be perfectly formed. With the excess dough, make a bread roll.

PROBLEM

Your bread collapses in the middle or droops over the sides of the tin; your bread has black spots on the top; when you cut your bread you see that the crumb has dropped, leaving a hole between the top of the crumb and the crust.

SOLUTION

You left your bread to prove for too long before baking.

When yeast runs out of puff it simply stops working. Bread that proves too long will collapse when it bakes. Simply put the dough on the counter, add a little more flour, knead gently, re-shape it and set it to rise again. Watch it carefully, though, as it will rise more quickly the second time around.

PROBLEM

Your bread is dense, brick-like and heavy.

SOLUTION

The refreshed starter was not ready. Or the dough was too dry. Or you have not proved the dough for long enough.

Make sure the refreshed starter is lively enough next time by doing the 'float' test (page 12).

Hydrate the dough a little more next time. Wetter dough moves more quickly and easily than dry dough and makes nicer bread.

Be patient: if you bake too soon, the dough will not have become as light as it could have done. This will lead to a heavy loaf.

PROBLEM

Your bread is sticky and under-baked when you cut into it.

SOLUTION

You have not baked the bread for long enough. Or you have added too much sour.

Make sure your dough is baked. If you are uncertain, buy a digital probe thermometer. When dough is ready it is 98°C.

If your 'sour' to 'flour' ratio is too high – this will not happen with any of the recipes in this book, but it can happen when you experiment – your bread will be a bit like clay on the inside. Reduce the percentage of refreshed sourdough.

PROBLEM

Your rye dough isn't rising.

SOLUTION

The refreshed starter was not ready. Or the dough was too dry. Or your kitchen was too cold.

Make sure the refreshed starter is lively enough next time by doing the 'float' test (page 12).

Hydrate the dough a little more next time. Wetter dough moves more quickly and easily than dry dough and makes nicer bread.

Be patient: if your refreshed starter was ready and your dough was nice and soft while kneading, it should be fine. Natural yeast is very sensitive to temperature. Simply keep it well covered with a shower cap and put it somewhere nice and warm (though not too warm): in the oven with the light on and the temperature off is good.

PROBLEM

Your rye bread is collapsing, even though you know it was not over-proofed.

SOLUTION

It's too hot to bake rye.

Rye loves cooler weather and performs in odd ways when the temperature is more than 26–27°C. If you are determined to bake rye when it's hot, allow it to rise for an hour or two and then put it in the fridge to complete the rise.

PROBLEM

Your bread is burning on the top before it is done.

SOLUTION

Check the bread 10 or 15 minutes before it is due to come out of the oven. If it is getting too brown, cover it with some non-stick baking parchment.

You may want to check that your oven is performing as it should. Use an oven thermometer to make sure it is the correct temperature.

PURE RYE

- -

This recipe produces a rich, dark loaf that is packed with flavour. As it contains only rye flour, it won't rise like a wheat loaf, and its dense structure means it's best served in thin slices.

INGREDIENTS

20 g rye sourdough starter (page 40)
300 g dark or light rye flour
260 g water
5 g salt
rye or oat flakes, to cover

✿ NOTE:

Once the loaf is in the proving basket, it can be kept in the fridge for up to 8 hours before baking.

✿ TIP:

Dark rye has the bran and the germ from the grain (like whole wheat); light rye does not (like white wheat). Light rye bread is lighter in both colour and texture than breads made with dark rye. You can, however, use dark and light rye interchangeably. To test these recipes, I used dark rye flour.

METHOD

Day one

1. Measure the sourdough starter into a large bowl and return any remaining starter to the vat in the fridge.
2. Add 60 g flour and 120 g water. Stir and cover with cling film, and leave on the counter for around 8 hours.

Day two

3. Measure 160 g of the refreshed rye starter into a large bowl and return the rest to the fridge.
4. Add the remaining flour, water, and the salt and stir well with a spoon. You do not need to knead this as the gluten in rye will not 'develop' further. The mixture will be sticky, but it should be soft enough that you can push your finger through it easily. If your dough feels grainy and rather dry, add water gradually, mixing it in by hand and feeling for a soft, but still manageable, texture.
5. Generously coat a 600 g round proving basket with rye or oat flakes to stop your dough from sticking to the basket. Any excess will just brush off.
6. Wet your hands and pick up the dough. Shape it into a little round to fit in the basket. Lay it on a floured surface and gently 'pat' oat flakes all over it – especially the sides. Gently put it in the basket, oaty side down, and cover with a shower cap. Leave it to rise for 3–5 hours. You will know it is ready when it is visibly larger and the surface is full of little holes.
7. Preheat the oven to 230°C and gently invert the dough onto a baking sheet lined with non-stick baking parchment. Place the dough in the oven and bake for 10 minutes. Reduce the heat to 200°C and bake for a further 30 minutes.
8. Remove from the sheet and leave to cool completely on a wire rack.

FINNISH RYE

The addition of malt syrup gives this dense rye loaf a rich, golden colour, but the white flour means it still has a fluffy texture. This is a 'daily' bread in Scandinavian countries.

INGREDIENTS

35 g rye sourdough starter (page 40)
100 g dark or light rye flour
185 g white wheat or spelt flour, plus extra for dusting
80 g water
100 g milk
50 g malt syrup (honey or agave)
6 g salt
butter or oil, for greasing

METHOD

Day one

1. Measure the sourdough starter into a large bowl and return any remaining starter to the fridge.
2. Add 25 g rye flour, 35 g wheat or spelt flour and 30 g water. Stir and cover with cling film, and leave on the counter for around 8 hours.

Day two

3. Add the remaining ingredients to the refreshed starter and knead well for 10 minutes.
4. Grease a baking tin.
5. With wet hands, pick up the dough and shape it into a small brick, then gently place it into the tin. Flour the top heavily.
6. Cover with a shower cap and leave to rise for 3–5 hours until it has nearly filled the tin.
7. Preheat the oven to 230°C. Place the dough in the oven and bake for 10 minutes. Reduce the heat to 200°C and bake for a further 30 minutes.
8. Remove from the tin and leave to cool completely on a wire rack.

>> *See steps on page 48*

5

6

Shape the dough with wet hands and gently place in a greased baking tin.

Prove at room temperature until the dough almost fills the tin.

8

Remove from the tin and cool on a wire rack.

SWEDISH LIMPA

Limpa is a rye bread flavoured with molasses, orange zest and spices. Many recipes replace the water with dark beer.

INGREDIENTS

35 g rye sourdough starter (page 40)
25 g dark or light rye flour
250 g white wheat or spelt flour
180 g water
50 g malt syrup (honey or agave)
5 g salt
1 tsp ground fennel
1 tsp caraway seeds
grated zest of 1 orange
butter or oil, for greasing

METHOD

Day one

1. Measure the sourdough starter into a large bowl and return any remaining starter to the fridge.
2. Add 25 g rye flour, 25 g wheat or spelt flour and 30 g water. Stir and cover with cling film, and leave on the counter for around 8 hours.

Day two

3. Add the remaining ingredients to the refreshed starter and knead well for 10 minutes.
4. Grease a baking tin.
5. With wet hands, pick up the dough and shape it into a small brick, then gently place it into the tin.
6. Cover with a shower cap and leave to rise for 3–5 hours until it has nearly filled the tin.
7. Preheat the oven to 230°C. Place the dough in the oven and bake for 10 minutes. Reduce the heat to 200°C and bake for a further 30 minutes.
8. Remove from the tin and leave to cool completely on a wire rack.

>> *See steps on page 50*

Everyday Rye

SWEDISH LIMPA

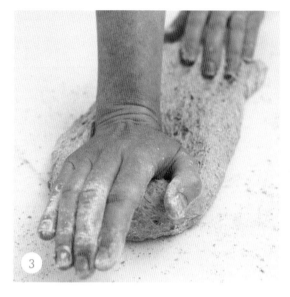

Knead well.

This will take about 10 minutes.

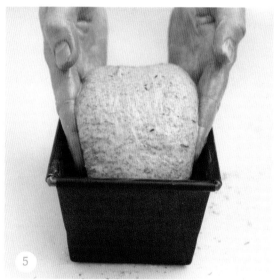

Shape the dough with wet hands into a small brick.

Gently place into a greased baking tin.

PEASANT BREAD

- -

The combination of coriander and molasses in this recipe demonstrates this bread's Russian heritage.

INGREDIENTS

55 g rye sourdough starter (page 40)
50 g dark or light rye flour
410 g whole wheat or spelt flour, plus
   extra for dusting
90 g water
200 g milk
50 g molasses
9 g salt
1 tsp ground coriander
50 g butter, lard or vegetable oil, plus
   extra for greasing

METHOD

Day one

1. Measure the sourdough starter into a large bowl and return any remaining starter to the fridge.
2. Add 50 g rye flour, 50 g whole wheat or spelt flour and 50 g water. Stir and cover with cling film, and leave on the counter for around 8 hours.

Day two

3. Add the remaining ingredients to the refreshed starter and knead well for 10 minutes.
4. Grease a ceramic or glass pie dish, or a 20 cm round baking tin or springform tin.
5. With wet hands, pick up the dough and shape it into a ball. Place it into the dish or tin, then gently flatten it into a disc. Don't try to fill the dish or tin; just flatten the ball. Generously flour the top.
6. Cover with a shower cap and leave to rise for 3–5 hours until it has nearly filled the tin.
7. Preheat the oven to 230°C. Place the dough in the oven and bake for 10 minutes. Reduce the heat to 200°C and bake for a further 30 minutes.
8. Remove from the tin and leave to cool completely on a wire rack.

>> *See steps on page 54*

Everyday Rye

PEASANT BREAD

Shape the dough into a ball.

Gently place it in a greased pie dish or baking tin.

Dust the loaf with flour.

Makes a 550 g loaf

PUMPERNICKEL RYE

Pumpernickel flour is a coarsely ground, dark rye flour. If you cannot find pumpernickel flour, just use regular dark rye flour.

INGREDIENTS

35 g rye sourdough starter (page 40)
75 g dark or light rye flour
200 g white wheat or spelt flour, plus
    extra for dusting
80 g water
100 g milk
50 g molasses
5 g salt
1 tsp caraway seeds
butter or oil, for greasing

METHOD

Day one

1. Measure the sourdough starter into a large bowl and return any remaining starter to the fridge.
2. Add 25 g rye flour, 25 g wheat or spelt flour and 30 g water. Stir and cover with cling film, and leave on the counter for around 8 hours.

Day two

3. Add the remaining ingredients to the refreshed starter and knead well for 10 minutes.
4. Grease a baking tin.
5. With wet hands, pick up the dough and shape it into a small brick, then gently place it into the tin. Generously flour the top.
6. Cover with a shower cap and leave to rise for 3–5 hours until it has nearly filled the tin.
7. Preheat the oven to 230°C. Place the dough in the oven and bake for 10 minutes. Reduce the heat to 200°C and bake for a further 30 minutes.
8. Remove from the tin and leave to cool completely on a wire rack.

 TIP:

Pumpernickel often contains seeds and grains. Try adding a handful of rye or wheat grains mixed with sunflower or pumpkin seeds. It is important to soak these overnight as the sourdough refreshes. To add them, simply drain and incorporate with all the other ingredients.

>> *See steps on page 56*

PUMPERNICKEL RYE

Prepare the starter and leave for 8 hours to refresh.

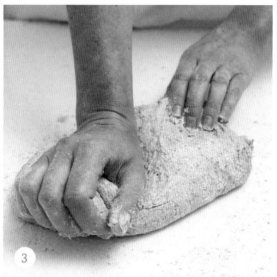

Knead well for 10 minutes.

Shape the dough with wet hands.

AUSTRIAN RYE

This is a lovely, light loaf with a delicate flavour, perfect for breakfast toast or sandwiches.

INGREDIENTS

100 g rye sourdough starter (page 40)
60 g dark or light rye flour
215 g wheat flour
20 g water
100 g milk
50 g malt syrup (honey or agave)
5 g salt
1 tsp caraway seeds
1 tsp ground coriander
½ tsp ground cumin
anise seeds, to cover
butter or oil, for greasing

METHOD

Day one

1. Measure the sourdough starter into a large bowl and return any remaining starter to the fridge.
2. Add 20g rye flour, 25 g wheat flour and all the water. Stir and cover with cling film, and leave on the counter for around 8 hours.

Day two

3. Add the remaining ingredients to the refreshed starter and knead well for 10 minutes.
4. Grease a baking tin.
5. With wet hands, pick up the dough and shape it into a small brick, then gently place it into the tin. Sprinkle anise seeds on the top.
6. Cover with a shower cap and leave to rise for 3–5 hours until it has nearly filled the tin.
7. Preheat the oven to 230°C. Place the dough in the oven and bake for 10 minutes. Reduce the heat to 200°C and bake for a further 30 minutes.
8. Remove from the tin and leave to cool completely on a wire rack.

DURUM RYE

- -

Durum flour, typically used to make pasta, has a very high gluten content. If you cannot find it, use the strongest bread flour you can find.

INGREDIENTS

65 g rye sourdough starter (page 40)
50 g dark or light rye flour
200 g durum flour
**165 g white wheat or spelt flour, plus
extra for dusting**
180 g water
50 g malt syrup (honey or agave)
7 g salt
50 g butter, lard or vegetable oil

METHOD

Day one

1. Measure the sourdough starter into a large bowl and return any remaining starter to the fridge.
2. Add 140 g durum flour and all the water. Stir and cover with cling film, and leave on the counter for around 8 hours.

Day two

3. Add the remaining ingredients to the refreshed starter and knead well for 10 minutes.
4. Cover the bowl with a shower cap and leave to rest for 1 hour on the counter.
5. Generously flour a medium-sized (around 800 g) oval proving basket.
6. Remove the dough from the bowl and place it on a floury work surface. With wet hands, gently stretch it out into a flat rectangle that is just a little narrower than your basket.

7. With the help of a scraper, fold the top edge to the middle and gently press along the seam. Fold the bottom edge to meet it and gently press along the seam. Still using the scraper, fold the dough in half lengthways and, with the heel of your hand, seal the long edge.
8. Sit the dough on the sealed seam and, using the sides of your hands, seal up both side edges.
9. Sprinkle flour over the dough and pick it up (it's more robust than it looks) and place it seam side up in the basket. Cover with a shower cap and leave to rest for 3–5 hours.
10. Preheat the oven to 230°C and gently invert the dough onto a baking sheet lined with non-stick baking parchment. Place the dough in the oven and bake for 10 minutes. Reduce the heat to 200°C and bake for a further 30 minutes.
11. Remove from the tin and leave to cool completely on a wire rack.

TIP:

Strong flour has a high gluten content and is milled from what is called 'hard wheat' that is planted in the spring. In Italy it is used to make the best-quality pasta. You may see flour that is labelled 'durum' flour, but if you don't you can buy flour that is labelled 'strong' or 'extra strong' bread flour.

RAISIN RYE

This is excellent bread for breakfast toast. It also pairs beautifully with cheese.

INGREDIENTS

130 g rye sourdough starter (page 40)

50 g dark or light rye flour

280 g white wheat or spelt flour, plus
   extra for dusting

135 g water

50 g honey

6 g salt

50 g butter

100 g raisins

For the glaze:

½ beaten egg

½ tbsp milk

METHOD

Day one

1. Measure the sourdough starter into a large bowl
   and return any remaining starter to the fridge.

2. Add 50 g rye flour and 60 g water. Stir and cover
   with cling film, and leave on the counter for
   around 8 hours.

3. Place the raisins in a bowl and cover with cold
   water. Set aside on the counter.

Day two

4. Add the remaining ingredients, except the raisins, to
   the refreshed starter and knead well for 10 minutes.

5. Cover the bowl with platic wrap ot a shower cap
   and leave to rest for 1 hour on the counter.

6. Generously flour a medium-sized (around 800 g)
   oval proving basket.

7. Drain the raisins.

8. Remove the dough from the bowl and place it
   on a floury work surface. With wet hands, gently
   stretch it out into a flat rectangle that is just a little
   narrower than your basket. Scatter the raisins over
   the top of your dough and gently press them into
   the dough.

9. With the help of a scraper, fold the top edge to the
   middle and gently press along the seam. Fold the
   bottom edge to meet it and gently press along the
   seam. Still using the scraper, fold the dough in half
   lengthways and, with the heel of your hand, seal the
   long edge.

10. Sit the dough on the sealed seam and, using the
    sides of your hands, seal up both side edges.

11. Sprinkle flour over the dough and pick it up (it's
    more robust than it looks) and place it seam side
    up in the basket. Cover with a shower cap and
    leave to rest for 3–5 hours.

12. Preheat the oven to 230°C and gently invert the
    dough onto a baking sheet lined with non-stick
    baking parchment. Combine the ingredients for
    the glaze and brush onto the loaf. Place the dough
    in the oven and bake for 10 minutes. Reduce the
    heat to 200°C and bake for a further 30 minutes.

13. Remove from the tin and leave to cool completely
    on a wire rack.

>> *See steps on pages 64–65*

RAISIN RYE

8

9

Stretch out the dough and gently press in the raisins.

Fold the dough in half lengthways.

9

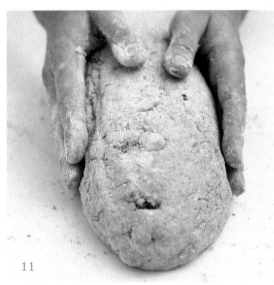

11

Seal the edges by firmly pinching.

Pick up the dough to transfer it to the proving basket

Place the loaf on a baking sheet.

Combine the ingredients for the glaze and brush onto the loaf.

❧ FAST FACT: READ THE LABEL

Not all bread that is sold as sourdough is 'pure' sourdough bread; it could be baked in an industrial process with the addition of sourdough powders that mimic the flavour of sourdough bread. Always read the label, ask the bakery and do your homework. A pure sourdough loaf will take most of a day to prepare and bake and will contain no commercial yeast.

Everyday Rye

CARAWAY SPELT

Spelt produces a rich, creamy texture and nutty flavour when added to a sourdough starter. The caraway seeds give this bread a wonderful flavour.

INGREDIENTS

130 g rye sourdough starter (page 40)

125 g dark or light rye flour

275 g whole or white spelt flour, plus extra for dusting

210 g water

50 g malt syrup (honey or agave)

8 g salt

50 g butter or lard

½ tsp caraway seeds

METHOD

Day one

1. Measure the sourdough starter into a large bowl and return any remaining starter to the fridge.

2. Add 25 g rye flour, 25 g spelt flour and 60 g water. Stir and cover with cling film, and leave on the counter for around 8 hours.

Day two

3. Add the remaining ingredients to the refreshed starter and knead well for 10 minutes.

4. Cover the bowl with a shower cap and leave to rest for 1 hour on the counter.

5. Generously flour a medium-sized (around 800 g) oval proving basket.

6. Remove the dough from the bowl and place it on a floury work surface. With wet hands, gently stretch it out into a flat rectangle that is just a little narrower than your basket.

7. With the help of a scraper, fold the top edge to the middle and gently press along the seam. Fold the bottom edge to meet it and gently press along the seam. Still using the scraper, fold the dough in half lengthways and, with the heel of your hand, seal the long edge.

8. Sit the dough on the sealed seam and, using the sides of your hands, seal up both side edges.

9. Sprinkle flour over the dough and pick it up (it's more robust than it looks) and place it seam side up in the basket. Cover with a shower cap and leave to rest for 3–5 hours.

10. Preheat the oven to 230°C and gently invert the dough onto a baking sheet lined with non-stick baking parchment. Place the dough in the oven and bake for 10 minutes. Reduce the heat to 200°C and bake for a further 30 minutes.

11. Remove from the tin and leave to cool completely on a wire rack.

EVERYDAY WHEAT

Here you'll find a recipe for San Francisco Sourdough (page 74), the best-known of all sourdough breads. Prepare the wheat starter on page 71 then try your hand at making this iconic loaf.

WHEAT BAKING BASICS

A BRIEF HISTORY OF WHEAT

Wheat is consistently one of the top three crops grown in the world, and the story of wheat, and how it came to be grown so widely and in such volume, is fascinating. The grasses from which modern wheat has been derived originated somewhere between what are now western Armenia and eastern Turkey. These 'goat grasses' were probably hybridised by early farmers as long as 10,000 years ago, improving their yields and their resistance to weather and insects. Over the millennia the grains they have produced include einkorn, emmer, spelt and the various strains of wheat that are grown today.

The story of wheat is the story of exploration and exodus. As humans have travelled, crops have spread, and wheat has proven itself to be a very adaptable crop. Wheat gluten is stretchy which means that bakers can shape wheat dough in many different ways to exercise their creativity and delight the eye.

GLUTEN

A great deal has been written in the past ten years about the rise of gluten intolerance. There is no doubt this is happening and that many people feel better when they stop eating wheat and other grains that contain gluten. What is not clear, however, is exactly why this is happening. What sourdough bakers know for sure is that people who suffer discomfort when they eat industrially produced bread, don't necessarily experience this when they eat long-fermented bread.

The gluten in wheat and its cousins (einkorn, emmer, spelt and kamut) is stretchy. 'Hard', 'strong' or 'high-protein' flour will make a dough that is very stretchy and strong, whereas 'soft', 'plain', 'cake and pastry' or 'low-protein' flour will make a dough that is more fragile. Bread made with hard flour will rise higher because the gluten will stretch out more

before it begins to collapse. It will also be chewier. Bread made with soft flour will not rise as much and will be softer in the mouth. People with coeliac disease cannot eat any gluten from any grain. People who do not tolerate wheat gluten often find they can tolerate spelt, emmer, einkorn or kamut flour – all of which are distant cousins to wheat.

SWITCHING FLOUR

You can substitute spelt, emmer, einkorn or kamut for wheat flour in any recipe, but remember that the texture of the dough, and the look, feel and taste of the final product, will be different. I suggest you follow recipes to the letter at first and try to memorise what the dough feels like – how sticky, how stretchy, how damp, etc. Then you can swap in different kinds of flour. Remember that different brands of flour, and different bags of the same brand, will vary and will require slightly different amounts of water to get the dough to the desired texture. Changing grains will mean you need to adjust the recipe and adjust your expectations about the look and taste of the bread.

KNEADING WHEAT BREAD

As you knead dough with wheat (or wheat family) flour, the dough transforms from a ragged mass to a stretchy, soft, pillowy delight. However, this usually takes a good 10 minutes or more of hard work. Remember that kneading is just stretching – like you stretch a balloon before you blow it up – and you need to stretch out your dough so the carbon dioxide created by the yeast can expand the dough more easily. A scraper will help you gather dough back after stretching it out.

You can knead any recipe in a machine and it will still take 10 minutes. You may need to stop the machine at several points in the process and, using a scraper, turn the dough over by hand.

MAKING A WHEAT SOURDOUGH STARTER

Day one

Mix 50 g white wheat flour and 50 g water together in a large bowl. Cover with cling film or place a dinner plate on top of the bowl and leave it on the counter for 24 hours.

Day two

Add 50 g white wheat flour and 50 g water to the mix in the bowl. Stir, cover it, and leave it on the counter for 24 hours.

Day three

Add 50 g white wheat flour and 50 g water to the mix in the bowl. Stir, cover it, and leave it on the counter for 24 hours.

Day four

Add 50 g white wheat flour and 50 g water to the mix in the bowl. Stir, cover it, and leave it on the counter for 24 hours.

Day five

Your starter should be bubbly – if it is, you have a viable starter. If not, don't add any more flour or water – just cover it and let it sit for another 24 hours. However, if nothing has happened by day six, it is unlikely that your starter will be a success this time around. Chalk it up to experience, rinse out the bowl and try again. Very occasionally, in some locations, the air is polluted and sadly lacking in natural yeast. Another uncommon (but entirely possible) reason is that your house is too clean.

READY TO BAKE

You now have plenty of starter to use straight away in any recipe that calls for a wheat starter. You also have plenty to put back into a container in the fridge to take out when you need it. When you get down to a small amount of starter in the fridge, simply top up the container. The refreshment ratio for a wheat starter is 1:1:1. Weigh the starter and add it to a large bowl with the same amounts of water and white wheat flour. Stir, cover, and leave for 8–12 hours. Your wheat sourdough starter is now topped up.

Day three · Day four · Day five

Your starter should be bubbly and lively; you will notice that small bubbles start to appear after a couple of days.

TROUBLESHOOTING WHEAT BREAD

PROBLEM
Your bread is dense, brick-like and heavy.
SOLUTION
The refreshed starter was not ready. Or the dough was too dry. Or you have not proved the dough for long enough.

Make sure the refreshed starter is lively enough next time by doing the 'float' test (page 12).

Hydrate the dough a little more next time. Wetter dough moves more quickly and easily than dry dough and makes nicer bread.

Be patient: if you bake too soon, the dough will not have become as light as it could have done. This will lead to a heavy loaf.

PROBLEM
Your bread is cracked along the side. The crack may be along the top of a loaf that you have baked in a tin, or along the bottom of a loaf that you have baked on a baking sheet.
SOLUTION
You have not proved the dough for long enough before putting it in the oven.

Dough springs up when it hits the heat of the oven and if your dough is not sufficiently relaxed it will crack rather than stretch. The dough should pass the 'probe' test (page 13) before baking.

PROBLEM
Your bread collapses in the middle or droops over the sides of the tin; your bread has black spots on the top; when you cut your bread you see that the crumb has dropped, leaving a hole between the top of the crumb and the crust.
SOLUTION
You left your bread to prove for too long before baking.

When yeast runs out of puff it simply stops working, and if this goes on for too long while the dough is rising, it will collapse when it bakes. If you leave it long enough, you will see the top of the dough beginning to sink. If you catch it, don't throw it away. Simply put the dough on the counter, add a little more flour, knead gently, re-shape it and set it to rise again. Watch it carefully, though, as it will rise more quickly the second time around.

PROBLEM

Your bread is burning on the top before it is done.

SOLUTION

Check the bread 10 or 15 minutes before it is due to come out of the oven. If it is getting too brown, cover it with some non-stick baking parchment.

You may want to check that your oven is performing as it should. Use an oven thermometer to make sure it is the correct temperature.

PROBLEM

Your bread has exploded out of the tin. It may develop a crack in the middle of the loaf on the top and explode out of that, or it will develop a crack along the side that completely separates the top of the loaf from its body.

SOLUTION

You have too much dough in your tin.

Limit the amount of dough to two-thirds of the tin. You may get a stumpy little loaf but at least it will be perfectly formed, and you know for next time that you can put more dough in the tin. With the excess dough, make a bread roll or buy some small tins (100 g) and bake the excess in them.

PROBLEM

Your bread is sticky and under-baked when you cut into it.

SOLUTION

You have not baked the bread for long enough. Or you have added too much sour.

Make sure your dough is baked. If you are uncertain, buy a digital probe thermometer. When dough is ready it is 98°C.

If your 'sour' to 'flour' ratio is too high – this will not happen with any of the recipes in this book, but it can happen when you experiment – your bread will be a bit like clay on the inside. Reduce the percentage of refreshed sourdough.

PROBLEM

Your wheat dough doesn't rise much in the time indicated by the recipe.

SOLUTION

The refreshed starter was not ready. Or the dough was too dry. Or your kitchen was too cold.

Make sure the refreshed starter is lively enough next time by doing the 'float' test (page 12).

Hydrate the dough a little more next time. Wetter dough moves more quickly and easily than dry dough and makes nicer bread.

Be patient: if your refreshed starter was ready and your dough was nice and soft while kneading, it should be fine. Natural yeast is very sensitive to temperature. Simply keep it well covered with a shower cap and put it somewhere nice and warm (though not too warm): in the oven with the light on and the temperature off is good.

SAN FRANCISCO SOURDOUGH

This is the best known of all sourdough breads and the one you're likely to see on display at farmers' markets and artisan bakers. It is fiddly if you want to do it 'right', but it's worth it.

INGREDIENTS

80 g wheat sourdough starter (page 71)
530 g white wheat flour, plus extra for
    dusting
370 g water
10 g salt

METHOD

Day one

1. Measure the sourdough starter into a large bowl and return any remaining starter to the fridge.
2. Add 80 g flour and 80 g water. Stir and cover with cling film, and leave on the counter for around 8 hours.

Day two

3. Add the remaining ingredients to the refreshed starter and knead well for 10 minutes. Put the dough in a bowl, cover with a shower cap and leave to rest for 6 hours. If possible, stretch and fold the dough every hour during that time. Simply pinch the edge of the dough, stretch it up and fold it over the rest of the dough. Don't press it down, just lay it down. Work your way around the edge of the dough, stretching and folding 4–6 times.
4. Turn the dough out onto a floury surface. Stretch and fold the dough once more and then shape into a ball. Flour the top generously and place it, floury side down, in a well floured 1 kg round proving basket. Cover with a shower cap and leave to rest for 2–4 hours or until it passes the 'probe' test.
5. Preheat the oven to 230°C. Invert the basket to roll the dough gently onto a baking sheet lined with non-stick baking parchment. Put the dough in the oven and bake for 10 minutes. Reduce the heat to 200°C and bake for a further 30 minutes.
6. Remove from the oven and leave to cool completely on a wire rack.

WHOLE WHEAT SOURDOUGH

A classic wholemeal loaf that is surprisingly light and very flavoursome.

INGREDIENTS

80 g wheat sourdough starter (page 71)
580 g whole wheat or spelt flour, plus extra for dusting
230 g water
200 g milk
11 g salt

METHOD

Day one

1. Measure the sourdough starter into a large bowl and return any remaining starter to the fridge.
2. Add 80 g flour and 80 g water. Stir, cover with cling film and leave on the counter for around 8 hours.

Day two

3. Add the remaining ingredients to the refreshed starter and knead well for 10 minutes. Put the dough in a bowl, cover with a shower cap and leave to rest for 4 hours.
4. Generously flour a 1 kg oval proving basket. Remove the dough from the bowl and place it on a floury work surface. Gently stretch it out into a flat rectangle just a little narrower than your basket.
5. With the help of a scraper, fold the top edge to the middle and gently press along the seam. Fold the bottom edge to meet it and gently press along the seam. Still using the scraper, fold the dough in half lengthways and, with the heel of your hand, seal the long edge.
6. Sit the dough on the sealed seam and, using the sides of your hands, seal up both side edges.
7. Sprinkle flour over the dough and pick it up (it's more robust than it looks) and place it seam side up in the basket. Cover with a shower cap and leave to rest for 2–3 hours or until it passes the 'probe' test.
8. Preheat the oven to 230°C. Invert the dough onto a baking sheet lined with non-stick baking parchment. Place the dough in the oven and bake for 10 minutes. Reduce the heat to 200°C and bake for a further 30 minutes.
9. Remove from the oven and leave to cool completely on a wire rack.

Everyday Wheat

MIXED GRAIN SOURDOUGH

This typical German loaf contains spelt and wheat. Filling and delicious, it is best enjoyed when thinly sliced.

INGREDIENTS

80 g wheat sourdough starter (page 71)
330 g white or whole wheat flour, plus extra for dusting
250 g white or whole spelt flour
430 g water
11 g salt

METHOD

Day one

1. Measure the sourdough starter into a large bowl and return any remaining starter to the fridge.
2. Add 80 g spelt flour and 80 g water. Stir and cover with cling film, and leave on the counter for around 8 hours.

Day two

3. Add the remaining ingredients to the refreshed starter and knead well for 10 minutes. Put the dough in a bowl, cover with a shower cap and leave to rest for 4 hours.
4. Generously flour a 1 kg oval proving basket. Remove the dough from the bowl and place it on a floury work surface. Gently stretch it out into a flat rectangle just a little narrower than your basket.
5. With the help of a scraper, fold the top edge to the middle and gently press along the seam. Fold the bottom edge to meet it and gently press along the seam. Still using the scraper, fold the dough in half lengthways and, with the heel of your hand, seal the long edge.
6. Sit the dough on the sealed seam and, using the sides of your hands, seal up both side edges.
7. Sprinkle flour over the dough and pick it up (it's more robust than it looks) and place it seam side up in the basket. Cover with a shower cap and leave to rest for 2–3 hours or until it passes the 'probe' test.
8. Preheat the oven to 230°C. Invert the dough onto a baking sheet lined with non-stick baking parchment. Place the dough in the oven and bake for 10 minutes. Reduce the heat to 200°C and bake for a further 30 minutes.
9. Remove from the oven and leave to cool completely on a wire rack.

'DO-GOOD' LOAF

This is a variation of a recipe that was developed by Dr Clive McCay at Cornell University, USA, in the 1940s. It was dubbed the 'Do-Good' Loaf by Jean Hewitt in the New York Times Sunday Magazine.

INGREDIENTS

65 g wheat sourdough starter (page 71)
125 g white wheat flour, plus extra for dusting
265 g whole wheat flour
65 g water
200 g milk
1 tbsp wheatgerm
7 g salt

METHOD

Day one

1. Measure the sourdough starter into a large bowl and return any remaining starter to the fridge.
2. Add 65 g whole wheat flour and all the water. Stir and cover with cling film, and leave on the counter for around 8 hours.

Day two

3. Add the remaining ingredients to the refreshed starter and knead well for 10 minutes. Put the dough in a bowl, cover with a shower cap and leave to rest for 4 hours.
4. Generously flour a medium-sized (800 g) round proving basket. Remove the dough from the bowl and place it on a floury work surface. Gently stretch and fold it once (see page 74) and shape into a ball .
5. Sprinkle flour over the dough and place it, floury side down, in the basket. Cover with a shower cap and leave to rest for 2–3 hours or until it passes the 'probe' test.
6. Preheat the oven to 230°C. Invert the dough onto a baking sheet lined with non-stick baking parchment. Place the dough in the oven and bake for 10 minutes. Reduce the heat to 200°C and bake for a further 30 minutes.
7. Remove from the oven and leave to cool completely on a wire rack.

Makes 8 pitta breads

PITTA BREAD

These soft, flat rounds with a pouch inside are produced throughout the Middle East, both commercially and in the home. Wrap them in a clean tea towel as you take them out of the oven to keep them soft. Eat as soon as possible after baking.

INGREDIENTS

70 g wheat sourdough starter (page 71)

520 g white wheat flour, plus extra for dusting

60 g whole wheat flour

380 g water

10 g salt

METHOD

Day one

1. Measure the sourdough starter into a large bowl and return any remaining starter to the fridge.

2. Add 70 g white wheat flour and 70 g water. Stir and cover with cling film, and leave on the counter for around 8 hours.

Day two

3. Add the remaining ingredients to the refreshed starter and knead well for 10 minutes. Put the dough in a bowl, cover with a shower cap and leave to rest for 4 hours.

4. Scrape the dough out onto a lightly floured surface. Lightly flour the top of the dough and then, using a scraper, divide the dough into eight pieces. You can use a scale to weigh them or just do it by eye.

5. Take each piece and gently pound it in the palm of your hand into a little disc no more than 2.5 mm thick. If you are sticking to the dough, simply flour it a bit more. Place the pieces on a baking sheet lined with semolina or non-stick baking parchment.

6. Flour the tops again and then cover loosely with cling film. Leave to rest for 2–3 hours or until they pass the 'probe' test.

7. Preheat the oven to 250°C (or as high as you can get it) and bake the pittas for 15–20 minutes, depending on how hot your oven is.

8. Remove from the oven and wrap in a tea towel until you are ready to eat them.

3

5

CIABATTA

- -

Ciabatta is made with a very soft, wet dough that can be tricky to handle. The shaping is almost like folding a slippery piece of cloth. Use plenty of flour at the shaping stages, and work quickly so the dough doesn't have time to stick to you, the counter or your scraper. The flour must be white wheat for this recipe.

INGREDIENTS

200 g wheat sourdough starter (page 71)
700 g white wheat flour, plus extra for
    dusting
430 g water
12 g salt

METHOD

Day one

1. Measure the sourdough starter into a large bowl and return any remaining starter to the fridge.
2. Add 300 g flour and 130 g water. Stir and cover with cling film, and leave on the counter for around 8 hours. It is a stiff paste so you will probably need to get in there with your hands to get it all together.

Day two

3. Add the remaining ingredients to the refreshed starter and knead well for 10 minutes. Put the dough in a bowl, cover with a shower cap and leave to rest for 4 hours. It will be ready when the dough has formed blisters on the top. Remember this can take a while if the kitchen is cold.
4. Heavily flour two thick cotton or linen tea towels and roll up the edges until you have about 25 cm between the two rolled edges. This will create a 'sling' in which the dough will sit (and be contained) while it is proving (see image on page 85).

5. Scrape the dough onto a heavily floured work surface. It will spread out naturally into a rectangle: don't stretch it out any further. Flour a scraper and divide the dough into two equal pieces.
6. Flour your hands and scraper. Slide the scraper under the short side of one of the rectangles of dough. Stretch it out and fold it over into the middle of the dough. Put the scraper under the other short side, stretch it out and fold it over the top of the dough – as if you were folding a sheet of A4 paper to go into an envelope. Place it on one of the tea towels. Repeat with the other rectangle of dough.
7. Flour the tops of the loaves, lightly dimple them with your fingers and cover loosely with a tea towel. Leave to rest for 1½–2 hours. The dough is soft so it will pass the 'probe' test as soon as you shape it but don't let that fool you. Just leave it to rest until it has visibly expanded.
8. Preheat the oven to 250°C. Put a large baking sheet in the oven to heat up. When the oven is ready, remove the tray and line it with non-stick baking parchment (use oven gloves to do this) or scatter a layer of semolina or polenta over it. Quickly transfer the loaves to the sheet flipping them over as you do to ensure the air bubbles are evenly distributed. Place the dough in the oven and bake for 15–20 minutes. During the first 10 minutes, spray the oven three times with a plant mister to increase the humidity.
9. Remove from the oven and leave to cool completely on a wire rack.

>> See steps on pages 84–85

CIABATTA

Transfer the dough to a large bowl.

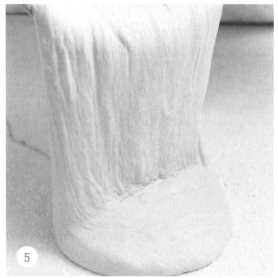

Transfer the dough to a well floured surface and flour the top.

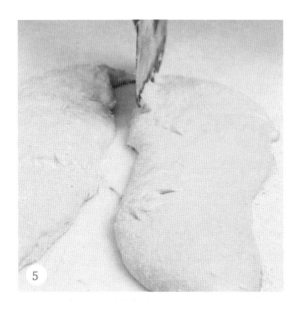

Using a dough scraper, divide into 2 pieces.

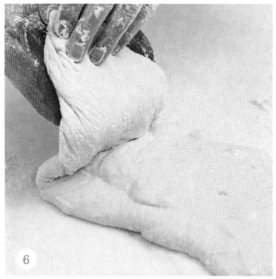

Pick up one edge (a scraper will help), and gently stretch it out and fold it into the middle of the rectangle.

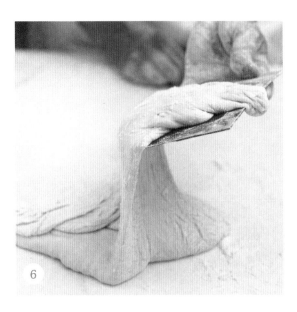

6

Take the other edge, gently stretch it out and fold it over the top of the rest of the rectangle.

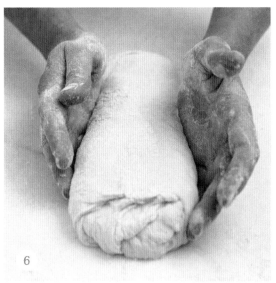

6

You should have what looks like a piece of folded A4 paper.

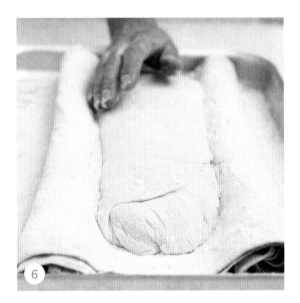

6

Carefully transfer the loaves to a heavily floured cloth.

✤ BAKING WHEAT BREAD

Wheat bread sounds 'hollow' when it is baked. In addition, the bottom crust feels 'thin' when you tap it. It will feel like you're tapping an empty plastic container; not one that is full of mashed potato. If you are concerned you won't get it right, buy a probe thermometer. The inside temperature of bread when it is baked is 98°C.

Finally, because sourdough bread dough is often more humid than 'regular' bread dough (wet dough rises more quickly and easily than dry dough and the relatively weak yeast in sourdough needs all the help it can get) your bread may be damper than you are used to. If it is, and you don't like it, wrap it in a tea towel and let it dry out for a day before you use it.

KAMUT BREAD

Kamut is a cousin of wheat. It is considered an ancient grain and the gluten is weaker than strong wheat flour, so don't expect a big rise or lots of strong stretchiness.

INGREDIENTS

40 g wheat sourdough starter (page 71)
240 g white wheat or spelt flour, plus extra for dusting
30 g kamut flour
25 g rye flour
200 g water
5 g salt

METHOD

Day one

1. Measure the sourdough starter into a large bowl and return any remaining starter to the fridge.
2. Add 40 g white wheat or spelt flour and 40 g water. Stir and cover with cling film, and leave on the counter for around 8 hours.

Day two

3. Add the remaining ingredients to the refreshed starter and knead well for 10 minutes. Put the dough in a bowl, cover with a shower cap and leave to rest for 4 hours.
4. Generously flour a 600 g round proving basket. Remove the dough from the bowl, place it on a floury work surface and shape it into a ball. Flour the top well and place the dough, floury side down, in the basket. Cover with a shower cap and leave to rest for 2–3 hours or until it passes the 'probe' test.
5. Preheat the oven to 230°C. Invert the dough onto a baking sheet lined with non-stick baking parchment. Place the dough in the oven and bake for 10 minutes. Reduce the heat to 200°C and bake for a further 30 minutes.
6. Remove from the oven and leave to cool completely on a wire rack.

DAILY BREAD

- -

This simple loaf is a go-to for breakfast toast and lunchtime sandwiches. The milk helps to produce a light, fluffy texture.

INGREDIENTS

30 g wheat sourdough starter (page 71)
260 g white wheat or spelt flour
90 g water
60 g milk
30 g honey
30 g butter
5 g salt
butter or lard, for greasing

METHOD

Day one

1. Measure the sourdough starter into a large bowl and return any remaining starter to the fridge.
2. Add 30 g flour and 30 g water. Stir and cover with cling film, and leave on the counter for around 8 hours.

Day two

3. Add the remaining ingredients to the refreshed starter and knead well for 10 minutes. Put the dough in a bowl, cover with a shower cap and leave to rest for 4 hours.
4. Grease a 500 g bread tin. Turn the dough out onto a floury work surface, shape it into a sausage and gently pop it into the tin. Cover with a shower cap and leave to rest for 2–3 hours or until it passes the 'probe' test.
5. Preheat the oven to 230°C. Place the tin in the oven and bake for 10 minutes. Reduce the heat to 200°C and bake for a further 30 minutes.
6. Remove from the oven and leave to cool completely on a wire rack.

Everyday Wheat

87

FRENCH BREAD

- -

Sourdough bread fell out of favour in French cities after the turn of the twentieth century when commercial yeast became available. However, it is now popular again and can be found at markets all over France.

INGREDIENTS

100 g wheat sourdough starter (page 71)
850 g white wheat flour, plus extra for
    dusting
550 g water
15 g salt

METHOD

Day one

1. Measure the sourdough starter into a large bowl and return any remaining starter to the fridge.
2. Add 100 g flour and 100 g water. Stir and cover with cling film, and leave on the counter for around 8 hours.

Day two

3. Add the remaining ingredients to the refreshed starter and knead well for 10 minutes. Put the dough in a bowl, cover with a shower cap and leave to rest for 4 hours.
4. Place a heavy cotton or linen tea towel on the counter and flour it heavily.
5. Scrape the dough out onto a floury surface and divide it into four pieces. Shape each one into a ball and flour the tops. Cover with cling film and leave to rest for 30 minutes.
6. Shape the balls into baguettes and lay them on the floury tea towel. Pleat the tea towel between each baguette so that each one is separated from the others. Flour the tops, cover with cling film and leave to rest for 2–3 hours or until they pass the 'probe' test.
7. Heat the oven to 230°C. Line a baking sheet with non-stick baking parchment or semolina. Transfer the baguettes to the baking sheet inverting them as you do so to ensure the bubbles are evenly distributed and slash across them a few times at an angle with a sharp knife or razor. Pop them in the oven and bake for 20–25 minutes.
8. Remove from the oven and leave to cool completely on a wire rack.

ENGLISH MUFFINS

Sourdough English muffins are the perfect accompaniment to Eggs Benedict. The sourdough makes them tangy and chewy, and they are delicious toasted.

INGREDIENTS

65 g wheat sourdough starter (page 71)
515 g white wheat or spelt flour, plus extra for dusting
165 g water
175 g milk
9 g salt
1 tsp bicarbonate of soda

>> *See steps on page 92*

METHOD

Day one

1. Measure the sourdough starter into a large bowl and return any remaining starter to the fridge.
2. Add 65 g flour and 65 g water. Stir, cover with cling film, and leave on the counter for around 8 hours.

Day two

3. Add the remaining ingredients, except the bicarbonate of soda, to the refreshed starter and knead well for 10 minutes. Put the dough in a bowl, cover with a shower cap and leave to rest for 4 hours.
4. Scrape the dough out onto a floury surface and sprinkle over the bicarbonate of soda. Do this through a sieve as it has a tendency to ball up and you really want it well distributed.
5. Gently knead the dough just to incorporate the bicarbonate of soda, then gently roll the dough into a disc about 2.5 cm thick. Scatter some semolina on the counter and place the dough on top. Flour the top of the dough with normal flour to prevent the cutter from sticking.
6. Using an 8 cm (or so) cutter with straight sides, cut out the muffins and flip them over onto a baking sheet lined with semolina. Cover with cling film and leave to rest for 2–3 hours or until they pass the 'probe' test.
7. Heat a frying pan to medium high and place the muffins in. Cook for 8 minutes on one side and then flip and cook for 8 minutes on the other side. The muffins are done when the internal temperature reaches 98°C.
8. Leave to cool completely on a wire rack.

Everyday Wheat

91

ENGLISH MUFFINS

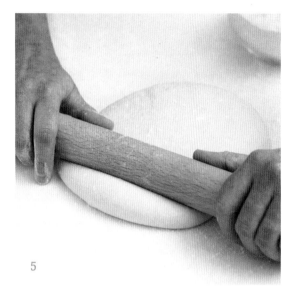

5

6

Gently roll out the dough on a floured surface into a disc that is approximately 2.5 cm thick.

Using an 8 cm cookie cutter, cut out the muffins.

6

Line a baking sheet with semolina. Place the muffins on the prepared sheet ready for proving.

BEIJING SESAME BUNS (SHAOBING)

Shaobing are traditional baked sesame buns that are crisp on the outside and tender on the inside. They are popular throughout northern and western China – you'll find them everywhere, from street vendors to high-end restaurants. You can buy sesame paste and Sichuan peppercorns at Chinese grocery shops. For a variation, replace the sesame paste with peanut butter.

INGREDIENTS

For the dough:
45 g wheat sourdough starter (page 71)
535 g white wheat flour
320 g water
10 g salt

For the filling:
1 tsp Sichuan peppercorns
½ tsp fennel seeds
3 tbsp roasted sesame paste
1 tbsp toasted sesame oil
pinch of salt
4 tbsp sesame seeds, to cover

METHOD

Day one

1. Measure the sourdough starter into a large bowl and return any remaining starter to the fridge.
2. Add 45 g flour and 45 g water. Stir, cover with cling film, and leave on the counter for around 8 hours.

Day two

3. Add the remaining ingredients to the refreshed starter and knead well for 10 minutes. The dough is typically quite dry so it may take some effort to knead. Put the dough in a bowl, cover with a shower cap and leave to rest for 3–4 hours.
4. Toast the Sichuan peppercorns and fennel seeds in a pan and grind to a powder. Place in a mixing bowl and add the remaining filling ingredients. If it is too dry, add more sesame oil – the consistency should be like a stiff syrup.
5. Turn out the dough onto a lightly floured surface, pat it into a rectangle and roll out until it is about 3 mm thick, and twice as long as it is wide. You will have to pause for the dough to rest, stretching it again with your hands, if necessary, and re-flouring the surface to prevent sticking.
6. Spread the sesame filling over the dough, leaving a 2.5 cm margin along one long side. Starting with the opposite edge, roll up the dough. Brush a little water on the margin and seal the roll.
7. Slice the dough into 7.5 cm rounds. Taking one segment, pinch each end closed, then stand it upright and gently flatten it into a disc, patting it out so that it is about 2 cm tall and 9 cm wide.
8. Place the sesame seeds on a plate. Brush each bun with water and gently press the top and bottom into the seeds. Leave to prove for 20 minutes.
9. Line a baking sheet with non-stick baking parchment. Place the buns on the sheet and bake at 180°C for 30 minutes. Best eaten fresh.

RECIPE BY SHELLEY JIANG

Born in Beijing, Shelley loves all things wheat-based, from steamed buns to flatbread to fried dough. As an editor of *The Insider's Guide to Beijing*, *Beijing by Foot* and *Beijing Eats*, Shelley has scoured Beijing for culinary treats. A trip to France in 2009 inspired her to bake bread from scratch, and she writes about food on her blog. Shelley currently lives in California. www.hawberry.net

MIXED GRAIN BREAD

- -

With its combination of wheat and spelt flours, and the addition of caraway and fennel seeds, this loaf is full of aromatic flavours – it will also smell wonderful while it bakes.

INGREDIENTS

40 g wheat sourdough starter (page 71)
125 g white wheat flour
125 g whole spelt flour
40 g white spelt flour
210 g water
25 g honey
5 g salt
½ tsp ground fennel
1 tsp caraway seeds

METHOD

Day one

1. Measure the sourdough starter into a large bowl and return any remaining starter to the fridge.
2. Add the white spelt flour and 40 g water. Stir and cover with cling film, and leave on the counter for around 8 hours.

Day two

3. Add the remaining ingredients to the refreshed starter and knead well for 10 minutes. Put the dough in a bowl, cover with a shower cap and leave to rest for 4 hours.
4. Grease a 500 g bread tin. Turn the dough out onto a floured surface and shape into a sausage. Pop the dough into the tin, cover with a shower cap and leave to rise for 2–3 hours or until it passes the 'probe' test.
5. Preheat the oven to 230°C. Place the tin in the oven and bake for 10 minutes. Reduce the heat to 200°C and bake for a further 30 minutes.
6. Remove from the oven and leave to cool completely on a wire rack.

FLAX PRAIRIE BREAD

When you need to increase your intake of omega-3, this is a good, inexpensive substitute to oily fish.

INGREDIENTS

40 g wheat sourdough starter (page 71)
140 g whole wheat flour
100 g white wheat flour
50 g ground flax
195 g water
25 g honey
5 g salt
sunflower seeds and flax seeds, to cover
butter or lard, for greasing

METHOD

Day one

1. Measure the sourdough starter into a large bowl and return any remaining starter to the fridge.
2. Add 40 g whole wheat flour and 40 g water. Stir and cover with cling film, and leave on the counter for around 8 hours.

Day two

3. Add the remaining ingredients to the refreshed starter and knead well for 10 minutes. Put the dough in a bowl, cover with a shower cap and leave to rest for 4 hours.
4. Grease a 500 g bread tin. Turn the dough out on to a floured surface, shape it into a sausage and gently pop it into the tin. Cover with a shower cap and leave to rise for 2–3 hours or until it passes the 'probe' test.
5. Spray the dough with water and sprinkle sunflower and flax seeds on top.
6. Preheat the oven to 230°C. Place the tin in the oven and bake for 10 minutes. Reduce the heat to 200°C and bake for a further 30 minutes.
7. Remove from the oven and leave to cool completely on a wire rack.

SOURDOUGH PIZZA BASE

A good base is essential for a great-tasting pizza. Leave plenty of space around the toppings, as the crust is deliciously chewy and crisp.

INGREDIENTS

60 g wheat sourdough starter (page 71)
140 g white wheat flour
1 tbsp fine semolina
90 g water
3 g salt
olive oil, for drizzling

TOPPING IDEAS:

- Mozzarella, cherry tomato, tomato sauce, garlic and herb oil
- Mushrooms, béchamel, halloumi, Parmesan
- Goats' cheese, capers, olives, chilli, caramelised onions, tomato sauce
- Chorizo, goats' cheese, roasted pepper, tomato sauce, mushrooms
- Sausage, mushroom, mozzarella, béchamel

METHOD

Day one

1. In a large bowl, mix together all the ingredients together to form a dough, do not knead. Drizzle olive oil over the dough, turning it to coat it completely. Cover the bowl with a shower cap and leave it on the counter to rest for 12-24 hours.

Day two

2. Line a baking sheet with non-stick baking parchment. Scrape the dough out onto the sheet and gently spread it out until it is as thin as you would like it to be. Leave to rest for 30 minutes.

3. Preheat the oven to 250°C (or as hot as you can get it). Top the pizza base with the toppings of your choice. Place the pizza in the oven and bake for 20–25 minutes, depending on how hot your oven is.

4. Slide the whole pizza (baking parchment and all) directly onto a wooden cutting board and use a pizza cutter to slice it.

BAGELS

Bagels are made with very stiff dough and are boiled before being baked. A great bagel will be chewy on the inside, crispy on the outside and full of flavour. It takes practice to get your perfect bagel, but the results will be delicious along the way.

INGREDIENTS

70 g wheat sourdough starter (page 71)
570 g white wheat flour, plus extra for dusting
180 g water
200 g milk
10 g salt
1 egg, beaten, for brushing
sesame seeds, to decorate

METHOD

Day one

1. Measure the sourdough starter into a large bowl and return any remaining starter to the fridge.
2. Add 70 g flour and 70 g water. Stir and cover with cling film, and leave on the counter for around 8 hours.

Day two

3. Add the remaining ingredients to the refreshed starter and knead well for 10 minutes. Put the dough in a bowl, cover with a shower cap and leave to rest for 4 hours.
4. Scrape the dough out onto a floury surface and divide it into ten pieces. Shape each piece into a ball. Flour the pieces, cover with cling film and leave to rest for 30 minutes.
5. Pick up each ball and pinch it with your thumb and first finger through the middle. Gently widen the hole using both hands and lay the dough on a baking sheet lined with a heavily floured tea towel.

Flour the tops, cover with cling film and leave to rest for 2–3 hours or until they pass the 'probe' test.

6. Preheat the oven to 220°C and bring a large saucepan of water to a gentle boil. Put the bagels into the water (as many as will fit comfortably) and simmer for 20 seconds or so. Remove them with a slotted spoon, drain them as best you can, and place on a baking sheet lined with non-stick baking parchment. Brush with the beaten egg and sprinkle sesame seeds on top.
7. Place the bagels in the oven and bake for 20 minutes.
8. Remove from the oven and leave to cool completely on a wire rack.

ADAPTED FROM A RECIPE BY DANNY GABRINER

Founder of Sour Flour, Danny Gabriner started baking in 2009 and soon decided to leave the tech industry to embrace the world of sourdough. Sour Flour is devoted to creating delicious, naturally fermented breads and educating anyone interested in how to bake bread. After just five years, Danny is well known in the San Francisco Bay Area for his high-quality sourdough loaves, his aromatic bread and pizza classes, and his generous weekly bagel giveaways (every Monday Sour Flour bakes and gives away hundreds of bagels as a way of connecting with the community). www.sourflour.org

FLAVOURED WHEAT

Adding extra ingredients to your bread gives a depth of flavour and transforms it from the flavour carrier to the main event. All of the breads here use the wheat starter found on page 71.

BAKING WITH EXTRA INGREDIENTS

Bread can include lots of other delicious ingredients like milk, yoghurt, eggs, butter, spices, nuts, fruit and even vegetables. It is important to remember that the only thing yeast really likes is sugar – add sugar to your dough and it will rise more quickly (this is the reason why most factory bread contains sugar).

If you add anything else to bread dough, it will slow down the yeast, and heavy ingredients such as grated carrot, nuts or fruit will also weigh down the dough. Even light ingredients such as powdered spices will slow the rise – as will the addition of eggs, fat or milk – the yeast simply doesn't like them.

When you add other ingredients to your dough – even dried herbs – it's a good idea to add them after you have kneaded the dough. This is simply because you will destroy the additional ingredients if you knead them into the dough for 10 minutes: fruit will turn into smeary blobs, olives will disintegrate, herbs will become particles and nuts will hurt your hands. So, knead your dough and put it back in the bowl to rest. After 30 minutes, measure the ingredients, place them on top of the dough and gently fold/squeeze/stretch the dough around the ingredients to ensure they stay intact and are distributed evenly throughout the dough. You can also add the extras at the end of the first rise. Don't worry about your dough, as it will recover; worry about the ingredients.

SOAKING DRIED FRUIT

It is a nice idea to soak dried fruit before you add it to your dough. Soaking softens the fruit, and it also means it won't suck all the moisture from the dough as the fruit rehydrates itself. To soak dried fruit, simply cover it with the liquid of your choice and leave it on the counter overnight. You can use water, juice, cold tea or coffee, or alcohol if you wish – red wine, brandy, rum, tequila… they all add a certain something to the dough! The ideal time to soak the fruit is while your starter is refreshing – that way, both will be ready to use the following day. Before you add the fruit, drain it and give it a good shake. Your dough will become slightly wetter for the incorporation of soaked fruit, but that's fine – don't be tempted to add more flour.

SOAKING GRAINS AND SEEDS

It's essential that you soak grains and seeds before adding them to your dough. This removes the natural pesticides that the grains and seeds produce, and enables you to digest them more easily. They will be softer in the mouth so you won't break your teeth, and they will not suck moisture from the dough as they hydrate themselves. To soak grains and seeds you must use liquid that is cold or at room temperature, otherwise you will 'cook' the grains and seeds and they will spoil. As with fruit, you can soak these ingredients in any liquid you like. When you drain them, rinse them, give them a good shake and add them to the dough. They are pretty robust so you don't have to worry about squashing them; you just need to make sure they are nicely distributed throughout the dough.

DRY-ROASTING NUTS

Dry-roasting nuts before adding them to the dough helps to bring out the oils in the nuts and thus enhances their flavour. Place the nuts in a dry frying pan and stir them constantly over a high heat for 2–3 minutes. When they start to turn a golden colour and you begin to smell them, remove them from the pan or they will continue to roast – they burn in a second so be careful. Allow them to cool completely

before adding them to the dough, or the heat will kill the yeast. You can add them in the same way you add soaked ingredients.

HERBS

You can add fresh or dried herbs to your dough. Knead the dough first, then add the herbs as you would anything else, once you have waited for the dough to rest. If you are adding fresh herbs, you may want to chop them before adding them.

COOKED VEGETABLES

A number of recipes call for sautéed onions in the dough, and for this you need to remember two things. The first is to let the cooked vegetables cool completely before you add them to the dough or they will kill the yeast. You can cook them while the sourdough refreshes and set them aside. Secondly, you should add them once the dough has relaxed, as you do with dried fruit. That way they will maintain their shape and texture to add definitive taste to your bread.

OTHER DELICIOUS THINGS

You can add almost anything to your dough – grated raw carrot, chopped raw onion, different kinds of cheese, olives, pepperoni, sun-dried tomatoes, chilli flakes... use your imagination to come up with combinations that sound good to you. As with any ingredient you add, you should knead the dough first and then gently fold in the additional ingredients.

KNEADING, RISING AND SHAPING

KNEADING

You can knead dough in a machine but it's better to knead by hand at first to familiarise yourself with the texture of the dough. The better you knead, the better the bread will be. That's because kneading activates the gluten, allowing it to expand and trap the air bubbles that form when the yeast does its work. To knead, you simply stretch the dough over and over again. You can do this in the air, you can pin it down with one hand and stretch it out with the other, or you can fold the dough and slap it down on the surface.

While you knead, you will see the dough change from a ragged mess to a slightly sticky, pillowy ball that you can pick up and stretch so thinly that you can see light through it before it tears (the windowpane test). You should do this with any high-wheat-content dough to check that you have kneaded for long enough (it is impossible with rye dough).

Don't be tempted to add more flour to the recipes – they may be stickier than you are used to but sticky is good. Sticky is also different from wet: some doughs are wet and sticky; others are rather dry and sticky. However, all sourdough doughs are sticky.

It is very hard to destroy dough if you are kneading by hand. However, if you are kneading in a machine at too high a speed for too long you can over-knead. If your dough suddenly begins to fall apart and look a bit like spongy cottage cheese in a pond, you have over-kneaded it and you have to throw it away.

Adding ingredients

If you want to incorporate ingredients like herbs, fruit, nuts or olives, you should knead the dough, then allow it to rest a while to soften up, and then add the extra ingredients. Then you put the dough back in the bowl to complete its first rise. The alternative is to add the ingredients at the end of the first rise.

When kneading you stretch the dough over and over again.

Rising (or fermenting or proving)

You need to let dough rise at various stages that will always be laid out in the individual recipes. Some recipes will instruct you to pop the dough straight in a baking tin once it's kneaded. Other recipes will instruct you to let the dough rise in the mixing bowl, and then complete a final rise in a tin, on a cloth or in a proving basket (or other container).

There are a few things to remember about the rising process, the main one being that sourdough

Flavoured Wheat

bread takes much longer to rise than bread made with commercial yeast. Your dough is ready for the oven if it passes the 'probe' test. Simply poke your dough gently but firmly with your finger. If your finger goes straight through the dough really easily, your dough has probably over-risen. However, if the indentation springs back completely within a minute, the dough is ready for the oven. This isn't scientific I'm afraid, but you will learn from experience.

Rising tips

1. If dough more than doubles in size during its final rise, it may collapse while it bakes. If your dough has clearly collapsed (or climbed straight out of the tin or basket) during the final rise, pull it out, give it a gentle knead with a bit more flour, reshape it, pop it back in the tin or basket and let it rise again. If you don't realise your dough has over-risen, one of the following may happen:
   • It may collapse in the oven.
   • It may spread out like a pancake when you take it out of its form (basket or bowl, etc) and put it on the baking sheet.
   • When you cut into the loaf, you may see that the crust has come away from the crumb, leaving a gap between the two.
   • You may see that the top of the loaf is mottled

with burned black spots where the crust has come away from the crumb in an irregular way.

2. If your dough has not risen enough in its final rise, it will split in the oven. It usually splits where the dough meets the heat source. In a tin, the split will be along the side of the loaf at the top. If you are baking on a sheet the split will be on the bottom of the loaf or along the side at the bottom.

Shaping

Shaping is the most difficult part of the bread baking process. Most people were not born knowing how to shape bread, any more than they were born knowing how to play the piano or string a tennis racket. Muscle memory is developed over time, and with very little practice you will see how easy shaping is – just be patient with yourself while you learn.

The 'science' behind baking is that your dough needs a closed surface structure in order to rise. If the surface of the dough looks like a sponge at a microscopic level, all the gas that the yeast is giving off will escape through the holes and the dough will not rise. If the surface of the dough looks like cling film (no holes at all) all the gas that the yeast is giving off will be trapped and the dough will expand just like a balloon.

Shaping into a basket

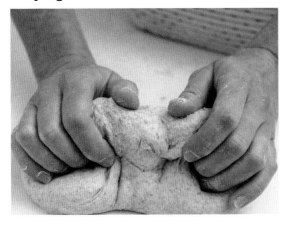 

Stretch and fold the dough into a tight sausage. Seal all the seams and place it seam side up in the basket. Turn it out of the basket so the seam is down on the baking sheet before baking.

Shaping wheat dough into a tin

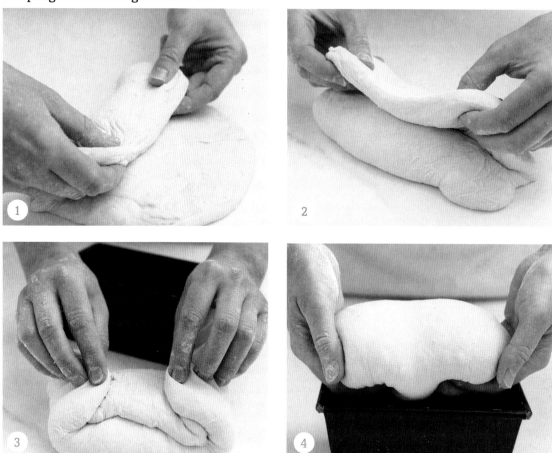

Stretch and fold the dough into a tight sausage. Place it seam side down in the tin.

The aim is to stretch the surface of the dough around itself in a thin membrane that will trap the gas that is given off by the yeast, and expand. When you are shaping sourdough bread, remember the yeast is not as powerful as commercial yeast, so you need to be gentle with your dough. You want to create the surface structure without taking all the air out of it. Here are a few points to remember:

- Dry dough is easier to shape. Put a light dusting of flour on your hands and use a floured scraper to help you move the dough around. Don't flour the table too much. Shaping is much easier if the dough sticks slightly to the surface. That way,

when you stretch it, you develop the tension.
- The baking tin is very forgiving when it comes to shaping. If you're uncertain, shape a simple sausage loaf and put it in a tin. The tin will contain your dough and prevent any unsightly bulges in your loaf that may result from imperfect shaping.
- The recipes give you guidance as to shaping but feel free to shape however you like. Remember: dough made with wheat flour is the most versatile when it comes to shaping. Dough made of wholemeal or other types of flour is more fragile.

Braiding dough

Divide the dough into three equal pieces (use a scale if you do not trust your eye). Braid the dough just like hair. If you are finding it hard, dust the pieces with flour before you braid them.

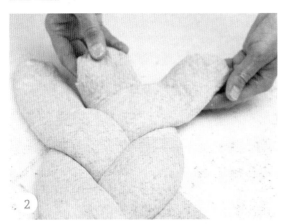

ONION AND OLIVE BREAD

- -

This delicious bread originates from Greece and Cyprus. Make sure the onion and olive mixture has cooled completely before adding it to the other ingredients.

INGREDIENTS

For the dough:
80 g wheat sourdough starter (page 71)
100 g whole wheat or spelt flour
480 g white wheat or spelt flour
380 g water
10 g salt

For the filling:
½ tbsp olive oil, plus extra for brushing
½ large onion, finely chopped
90 g black or green olives (rinsed well
    if packed in brine), pitted and finely
    chopped

the onions for 8 minutes. Add the olives, give them a good stir and set aside to cool completely.

5. Scrape the dough out onto a floury surface and flatten it into a rectangle, about 40 x 25 cm. Scatter the onion and olive mixture evenly over the surface. Brush the edges with water, roll the dough up into a tight roll and then seal both ends and tuck them under the loaf.

6. Place the roll on a baking sheet lined with non-stick baking parchment. Brush the top with olive oil and then cover with a shower cap and leave to rest for 2 hours or until it passes the 'probe' test.

7. Preheat the oven to 230°C. Make several diagonal slashes in the top of the dough, then place the loaf in the oven and bake for 10 minutes. Reduce the heat to 200°C and bake for a further 30 minutes.

8. Remove from the oven and leave to cool completely on a wire rack.

METHOD

Day one

1. Measure the sourdough starter into a large bowl and return any remaining starter to the fridge.

2. Add 80 g flour and 80 g water. Stir and cover with cling film, and leave on the counter for around 8 hours.

Day two

3. Add the remaining dough ingredients to the refreshed starter and knead well for 10 minutes. Put the dough in a bowl, cover it with a shower cap and leave to rest for 3–4 hours.

4. Heat the olive oil in a frying pan and gently sweat

5

SPELT AND WHEAT BREAD WITH HERBS

This is a beautiful, plain loaf that is great for sandwiches.

INGREDIENTS

35 g wheat sourdough starter (page 71)
160 g whole spelt flour
125 g white spelt flour
185 g water
5 g salt
**½ tsp each of dried thyme, oregano and
      basil**
milk, for brushing

METHOD

Day one

1. Measure the sourdough starter into a large bowl and return any remaining starter to the fridge.
2. Add 35 g whole spelt flour and 35 g water. Stir and cover with cling film, and leave on the counter for around 8 hours.

Day two

3. Add the remaining ingredients to the refreshed starter and knead well for 10 minutes. Put the dough in a bowl, cover with a shower cap and leave to rest for 3–4 hours.
4. Scrape the dough onto a floured surface and shape it into a tight sausage. Pop it into a greased 500 g baking tin and cover with a shower cap. Leave it to rest for 2 hours or until it passes the 'probe' test.
5. Preheat the oven to 230°C. Brush the top of the loaf with milk, then place it in the oven and bake for 10 minutes. Reduce the heat to 200°C and bake for a further 30 minutes.
6. Remove from the oven and leave to cool completely on a wire rack.

ROSEMARY BREAD

Fresh rosemary gives this distinctive round loaf a wonderful aroma and flavour, while the raisins add a hint of sweetness.

INGREDIENTS

 ----

80 g wheat sourdough starter (page 71)
580 g white wheat or spelt flour, plus
    extra for dusting
255 g water
150 g milk
30 g honey (or agave)
30 g butter or lard
10 g salt
1 tsp chopped fresh rosemary
1 egg
50 g raisins

For the glaze:
1 egg, beaten with 1 tsp water and a
    pinch each of salt and sugar

METHOD

Day one

1. Measure the sourdough starter into a large bowl and return any remaining starter to the fridge.
2. Add 80 g flour and 80 g water. Stir and cover with cling film, and leave on the counter for around 8 hours.
3. Place the raisins in a bowl and cover with cold water. Leave them to soak until you need them.

Day two

4. Add the remaining ingredients, except the raisins, to the refreshed starter and knead well for 10 minutes. Put the dough in a bowl, cover with a shower cap and leave to rest for 3–4 hours.
5. Drain the raisins and tip them on to the top of the dough. Gently squish them into the dough, leaving both the dough and the raisins as intact as possible.
6. Scrape the dough onto a floured surface and shape it into a ball. Flour the top and pop it, floury side down, into a heavily floured 1 kg round proving basket. Cover with a shower cap and leave to rise for 2 hours or until it has passed the 'probe' test.
7. Preheat the oven to 230°C. Invert the basket, gently rolling the dough onto a baking sheet lined with non-stick baking parchment. Brush the glaze all over the dough. Slash the dough in a criss-cross pattern and place it in the oven for 10 minutes. Reduce the heat to 200°C and bake for a further 30 minutes; cover the dough with greaseproof paper or foil halfway through the cooking time so the raisins do not burn.
8. Remove from the baking sheet and leave to cool completely on a wire rack.

SUNFLOWER BREAD

Sunflower seeds, milk and honey make this the perfect breakfast loaf.

INGREDIENTS

80 g wheat sourdough starter (page 71)
330 g whole wheat or spelt flour
250 g white wheat or spelt flour
305 g water
100 g milk
50 g honey (or agave)
50 g butter or lard
70 g sunflower seeds, plus extra to decorate
10 g salt

METHOD

Day one

1. Measure the sourdough starter into a large bowl and return any remaining starter to the fridge.
2. Add 80 g whole wheat or spelt flour and 80 g water. Stir and cover with cling film, and leave on the counter for around 8 hours.
3. Place the sunflower seeds in a bowl and cover with cold water. Leave them to soak until needed.

Day two

4. Drain the sunflower seeds and rinse them well. Add them, along with all the other remaining ingredients, to the refreshed starter. Knead well for 10 minutes. Put the dough in a bowl, cover with a shower cap and leave to rest for 3–4 hours.
5. Scrape the dough onto a floured surface and shape it into a sausage. Flour the top and pop it, floury side down, into a heavily floured 1 kg oval proving basket. Cover with a shower cap and leave to rise for 2 hours or until it has passed the 'probe' test.
6. Preheat the oven to 230°C. Invert the basket, gently rolling the dough onto a baking sheet lined with non-stick baking parchment.
7. Spray water onto the loaf with a plant mister and sprinkle sunflower seeds on top. Then spray the loaf again to make sure they stick. Slash the top of the loaf diagonally a few times and pop it in the oven for 10 minutes. Reduce the heat to 200°C and bake for a further 30 minutes; after 20 minutes, cover the dough with some greaseproof paper or foil so the sunflower seeds do not burn.
8. Remove the bread from the oven and leave to cool completely on a wire rack.

CHEESE AND ONION BREAD

Adding freshly chopped spring onion to cheese bread yields a truly delicious loaf.

INGREDIENTS

For the dough:
80 g wheat sourdough starter (page 71)
580 g white wheat or spelt flour, plus
    extra for dusting
305 g water
60 g milk
50 g butter or lard, plus extra for
    brushing
10 g salt

For the filling:
100 g spring onions, finely chopped
200 g mature Cheddar cheese, grated

To glaze:
1 egg, beaten with 1 tsp water and a
    pinch of salt

METHOD

Day one

1. Measure the sourdough starter into a large bowl and return any remaining starter to the fridge.
2. Add 80 g flour and 80 g water. Stir and cover with cling film, and leave on the counter for around 8 hours.

Day two

3. Add the remaining dough ingredients to the refreshed starter and knead well for 10 minutes. Put the dough in a bowl, cover with a shower cap and leave to rest for 3–4 hours. Sprinkle the onions and cheese on top of the dough and gently squish them into the dough, leaving both the dough and the onions and cheese as intact as possible.
4. Scrape the dough onto a floury surface and divide it into three pieces (you can weigh them out or just do it by eye). Roll each piece into a long sausage, about 3 cm in diameter, and flour each one lightly. Form them into a plait and then pinch the ends and fold them under. Place the dough on a baking sheet lined with non-stick baking parchment.
5. Brush some melted butter or olive oil on top of the dough and cover it with a shower cap. Leave it to rest for 2 hours or until it passes the 'probe' test.
6. Preheat the oven to 230°C. Brush the glaze over the top of the dough and pop it in the oven for 10 minutes. Reduce the heat to 200°C and bake for a further 30 minutes.
7. Remove from the oven and leave to cool completely on a wire rack.

RYE AND ONION LOAF

Onions and rye flour fuse to create a wonderful flavour combination. This recipe uses chopped onions lightly sautéed in butter, but raw chopped onions work equally well.

INGREDIENTS

For the dough:
70 g wheat sourdough starter (page 71)
70 g white wheat or spelt flour
325 g whole wheat or spelt flour
75 g dark or light rye flour
350 g water
8 g salt

For the filling:
1 tbsp butter
1 medium onion, chopped

METHOD

Day one

1. Measure the sourdough starter into a large bowl and return any remaining starter to the fridge.
2. Add all the white flour and 70 g water. Stir and cover with cling film, and leave on the counter for around 8 hours.
3. Heat the butter in a frying pan and gently sweat the onions for 8 minutes. Set them aside until needed.

Day two

4. Add the remaining dough ingredients to the refreshed starter and knead well for 10 minutes. Put the dough in a bowl, cover with a shower cap and leave to rest for 3–4 hours. Place the sweated onions on top of the dough and gently incorporate them, leaving the dough and the onions as intact as possible.
5. Scrape the dough onto a floury surface and shape it into a sausage. Flour the top and pop it, floury side down, into a heavily floured 1 kg oval proving basket. Leave to rest for 2 hours or until it passes the 'probe' test.
6. Preheat the oven to 230°C. Gently invert the basket, rolling the dough out onto a baking sheet lined with non-stick baking parchment. Using scissors, snip the dough, making a zigzag pattern down its length (don't do this with a knife as the dough is fragile and may pucker). Place the dough in the oven and bake for 10 minutes. Reduce the heat to 200°C and bake for a further 30 minutes.
7. Remove from the oven and leave to cool completely on a wire rack.

Flavoured Wheat

BACON, CHEDDAR AND JALAPEÑO LOAF

This bread came about from a trip to the farmers' market. The variety of jalapeño I bought was hotter than I was used to but I enjoyed the spice that came with it – if you like the heat, leave the seeds in. This makes a great sandwich with extra flavour added from the ingredients in the bread.

INGREDIENTS

For the dough:
60 g wheat sourdough starter (page 71)
480 g white wheat or spelt flour, plus extra for dusting
320 g water
8 g salt

For the filling:
50 g mature Cheddar cheese, cubed
3 slices cooked streaky bacon, chopped
1 large fresh jalapeño pepper, with stalks, seeds and veins removed, finely chopped

ADAPTED FROM A RECIPE BY DERIK HILL

Derik Hill first became interested in baking when he tried making pizza at home. This led him to other baking experiments and then to sourdough bread. Now he bakes several times a week and is constantly searching for the perfect loaf.
www.houseofbakes.com

METHOD

Day one

1. Measure the sourdough starter into a large bowl and return any remaining starter to the fridge.
2. Add 60 g flour and 60 g water. Stir and cover with cling film, and leave on the counter for around 8 hours.

Day two

3. Add the remaining dough ingredients to the refreshed starter and knead well for 10 minutes. Put the dough in a bowl, cover with a shower cap and leave to rest for 3–4 hours. Sprinkle the filling ingredients on top of the dough and gently fold them in, leaving the dough and fillings as intact as possible.
4. Scrape the dough onto a floury surface and shape it into a sausage. Flour the top and place it, floury side down, into a heavily floured 1 kg oval proving basket. Leave to rest for 2 hours or until it passes the 'probe' test.
5. Preheat the oven to 230ºC. Gently invert the basket, rolling the dough onto a baking sheet lined with non-stick baking parchment. Pop the dough in the oven and bake for 10 minutes. Reduce the heat to 200ºC and bake for a further 30 minutes.
6. Remove from the oven and leave to cool completely on a wire rack.

PLOUGHMAN'S SOURDOUGH

- -

I love food that is multi-functional – in other words, not only really tasty, but also healthy and nutritious. This particular sourdough ticks all those boxes. Practically a meal in itself, this loaf is one of my bestsellers at the markets. It's fantastic toasted and eaten with cold meats or a selection of cheese and pickles.

INGREDIENTS

For the dough:
100 g wheat sourdough starter (page 71)
600 g white wheat flour
100 g water
240 g dark ale or stout
10 g salt

For the filling:
1 eating apple, skin-on, cored and
    roughly chopped
2 handfuls chopped walnuts
1 tbsp chutney
2 handfuls grated mature Cheddar
    cheese

ADAPTED SLIGHTLY FROM A RECIPE BY VICKY MANNING

Vicky was never a fussy eater as a child and was an enthusiastic helper in the kitchen. She has always enjoyed making her own bread but only discovered sourdough last year. She started experimenting and in February 2014 decided to try some markets around Glasgow to see if people would be interested in buying her bread. They were and Vicky remains ecstatic. www.thelittlesourdoughbakery.co.uk

METHOD

Day one

1. Measure the sourdough starter into a large bowl and return any remaining starter to the fridge.
2. Add 100 g flour and all the water. Stir and cover with cling film, and leave on the counter for around 8 hours.

Day two

3. Add the remaining dough ingredients to the refreshed starter and knead well for 10 minutes. Place the dough in an oiled plastic container, cover with a shower cap and prove at room temperature for 6–8 hours until the dough has doubled in size.
4. Tip the dough onto a floured surface and stretch it into a round, flat shape. Place the filling ingredients on the dough and fold it over. Gently press the dough until all the ingredients are well incorporated.
5. Divide the dough in half and shape each half into a ball. Flour the tops and place floury side down into floured proving baskets. Leave, uncovered, at room temperature for 2–4 hours. The loaves are ready to bake when they have doubled in size and feel springy to touch when gently pressed. If your house is particularly warm, it may take less time to prove the loaves, so keep an eye on them.
6. Preheat the oven to 220°C. Gently tip the loaves onto preheated baking stones and bake for about 40 minutes. Place a tray of water in the bottom of the oven to prevent the loaves becoming too hard on the outside. Once baked, the loaves will sound hollow when tapped underneath.
7. Remove from the oven and cool on a wire rack.

Flavoured Wheat

123

SWEET BREAD AND BUNS

Sweet bread is a delicious alternative to cake. The results look (and taste) impressive, and the recipes you'll find here use the same basic skills as the more simple recipes in the book.

SWEET SOURDOUGH BASICS

Sweet bread and buns used to be baked for special occasions – high days, holidays, weddings and other celebrations. The simple reason for this was that the extra ingredients that make these recipes special used to be very expensive. Eggs, butter and milk are the usual enriching items that make the crumb soft and the flavour rich. Sugar, spices, dried fruit and nuts add to the special nature of this category of bread. Today, we can buy most ingredients most of the time, but it's fun to have some delicious, rich bread and bun recipes up your sleeve to bake for a special occasion.

Yeast

Yeast – natural or manufactured – is fussy and it only really likes sugar and water. Ingredients such as milk, eggs, butter, spices, fruit and nuts weigh down the dough and slow down the yeast. Sourdough bread does tend to be a little heavier and chewier than bread baked with yeast, but there are many ways to ensure your sweet bread and buns are light and delicious. You do not have to follow these directions to the letter, as they can be quite fiddly and time consuming, but they will help you achieve lighter, fluffier bread.

Baking basics

Make a pre-dough (also called a pre-ferment or flying ferment).

1. Measure the flour you need for the final dough into a large bowl and make a well in it. Measure the refreshed sourdough (amount stated in the recipe) into the well.
2. Measure the sugar and the liquid into the well.
3. Flick flour over the top of your well to close it and cover the bowl with a tea towel. Let it sit for a couple of hours and you will see that it becomes frothy.
4. Add all the remaining ingredients in the recipe and follow the instructions.

Creating pre-dough increases the yeast activity so,

when it comes to adding the things the yeast doesn't like, you have maximised the yeast's power.

Add butter last

Flour has an amazing ability to absorb fat and you want the flour to absorb the butter in its 'whole state'. Butter is an emulsion, and you don't want it to melt before the flour has absorbed it – once it has melted you can't put it back together again. The heat from your hands can melt the butter, and to avoid this you should knead the dough for a good 10 minutes and then add the butter (cold and cut into small pieces). Then knead again for another 10 minutes or so. The more butter there is, the more messy the job, but don't panic – use a scraper and keep going. The flour will absorb all the butter and your dough will turn a dark yellow colour and look and feel a bit like chewing gum.

Heat the milk and cool it down again

When you take milk to boiling point (watch the pan carefully as over-boiled milk is messy) you break down certain enzymes. This not only changes the flavour and the texture of the milk, it also makes the milk less able to hold back the yeast. Just make sure you cool the milk right down before adding it, so you don't kill the yeast in the sourdough. You can heat

the milk, return it to the fridge and add it cold to the recipe, if that works better for you. Waiting is boring, and if you are too impatient you might be tempted to add it when it is too hot.

Don't panic at the soft dough

Sweet bread and bun dough tend to be much softer than regular bread dough. At first this can be intimidating and you might think you have done something wrong. However, it's unlikely you have, so don't be tempted to add any more flour until you have tried a recipe at least a couple of times. You will quickly come to love working with soft dough.

TROUBLESHOOTING
SWEET DOUGH

PROBLEM
Your sweet dough doesn't rise much in the time indicated by the recipe.

SOLUTION
Natural yeast is particularly sensitive to hot and cold, and the difference of just a few degrees in room temperature could change your rising time from 3 hours to 5 or 6 hours. The timings assume 'room temperature' to be 24°C, so they are approximate. Sweet dough is ready for the oven when it has risen by one-and-a-half times – sourdough bread rarely rises more than that.

Sweet dough recipes, with their high-enriching ingredients such as butter, eggs, spices, dried fruit and nuts, can be even slower to rise than regular sourdough bread. All these ingredients slow down the rising process, so be patient if your kitchen is cool.

Use the 'probe' test to check if your bread is ready for the oven. Poke the dough gently with your finger to make an indentation: if your finger goes straight through, your bread is over-proved; if the indentation remains for a minute or more, the bread should prove for a little longer. If the indentation springs back within a minute, it is ready for the oven.

PROBLEM

Your bread or buns crack at the bottom where the dough hits the heat source.

SOLUTION

You have not let the dough rise for long enough. Enriched dough can take hours to rise so be patient – your dough will rise but it may take some time. Butter, milk, eggs, nuts and fruit all slow down the dough's fermentation. The 'probe' test (see opposite) works for sweet bread and buns too.

PROBLEM

Your bread or buns have a mottled top with little burnt spots, or the surface has collapsed altogether.

SOLUTION

The dough has risen too much. If you do not catch the dough 'on the turn' you will allow it to rise too much, and the dough will collapse in the oven or the crust will come away from the crumb, something you will only see when you cut into it. It can be hard to spot so chalk it up to experience and try again.

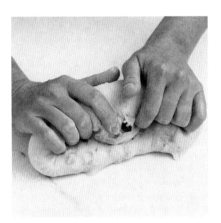

PROBLEM

You are having trouble shaping the soft, sticky dough.

SOLUTION

Shaping soft dough is tricky but avoid adding more flour to the dough, or over-flouring the counter. What you can do is have a bowl of flour to hand, and dip your hands in the flour, making your palms and the edges of your hands floury. This will enable you to handle and shape the dough with minimal stickiness. A scraper will also help enormously.

Do the first rise overnight or all day in the fridge. It is much easier to shape soft dough when it is cold. Leave the dough at room temperature for 1–2 hours before placing in the fridge, just to get it going. After shaping, it will take at least 8 hours to do a second rise from cold.

Sweet Breads and Buns

CINNAMON ROLLS

- -

A delicious, rich loaf that consists of individual spice-scented rolls. These come together during baking but can be gently pulled apart again to eat.

INGREDIENTS

For the dough:
55 g wheat sourdough starter (page 71)
455 g white wheat or spelt flour, plus
    extra for dusting
55 g water
220 g milk
50 g sugar
50 g butter, at room temperature, cubed,
    plus extra for greasing
8 g salt

For the filling:
50 g plus another 20 g butter, melted and
    cooled to room temperature
50 g brown sugar
1 tsp cinnamon
40 g walnuts or raisins, chopped into
    small pieces. Soak raisins for 10
    minutes before chopping

For the glaze (optional):
1 tbsp melted butter
50 g icing sugar
2 tsp milk
¼ tsp vanilla extract

METHOD

Day one

1. Measure the sourdough starter into a large bowl and return any remaining starter to the fridge.

2. Add 55 g flour and all the water. Stir and cover with cling film, and leave on the counter for around 8 hours.

Day two

3. Add the remaining dough ingredients to the refreshed starter and knead well for 10 minutes. Put the dough in a bowl, cover with a shower cap and leave to rest for 4 hours.

4. Scrape the dough onto a heavily floured surface and lightly flour the top. Use a rolling pin to shape it into a rectangle, abour 40 x 25 cm. Brush 50 g of the butter all over the surface of the dough and then sprinkle the sugar, cinnamon and walnuts or raisins over the top evenly. Roll the dough up from one of the long ends, using a scraper to help you. Place it seam side down on the counter and slice the dough into 12 equal pieces.

5. Snuggle the pieces of dough into a well buttered round cake tin, 45 cm or so in diameter. Brush the remaining butter over the tops and sides of the buns. Cover with cling film and let the dough rest for 2 hours or until it passes the 'probe' test.

6. Preheat the oven to 200°C. Place the buns in the oven and bake for 40 minutes, covering them with greaseproof paper or foil after 30 minutes so they do not burn.

7. Remove them from the tray with a spatula and let them cool completely on a wire rack.

8. If you would like to glaze them, mix the glaze ingredients together and then, with a spoon, dribble the glaze all over the tops of the buns.

>> See steps on page 132

CINNAMON ROLLS

Sprinkle the fillings over the dough.

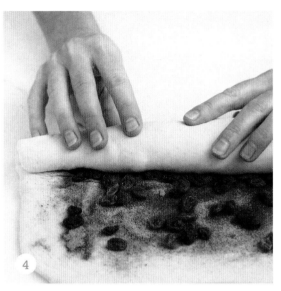

Roll up the rectangle from the long side.

Slice the dough into 12 equal pieces.

Place the slices in a greased round cake tin.

GINGERBREAD

Baking powder helps to leaven this delicious bread so no additional proving is required.

INGREDIENTS

65 g wheat sourdough starter (page 71)
345 g white wheat or spelt flour
65 g water
100 g butter, melted and cooled to room
   temperature, plus extra for greasing
60 g molasses
100 g milk
pinch of salt
1 egg
1 tsp ground cinnamon
1 tsp ground ginger
¾ tsp baking powder

METHOD

Day one

1. Measure the sourdough starter into a large bowl and return any remaining starter to the fridge.
2. Add 65 g flour and all the water. Stir and cover with cling film, and leave on the counter for around 8 hours.

Day two

3. In a large mixing bowl, whisk the butter, molasses, milk, salt and egg together. Add to the refreshed sourdough and mix well. In a separate bowl, sift together the remaining flour, spices and baking powder. Sift this into the bowl with the 'wet' ingredients. Stir or whisk to eliminate any lumps but don't over mix. The batter is thick, but if it's too thick you can slacken it with a drop of milk.
4. Scrape the batter into a 20 x 20 cm greased baking tin. Cover the tin with a shower cap and leave to rest for 3 hours.
5. Preheat the oven to 200°C. Place the loaf in the oven and bake for 40 minutes. Insert a knife into the centre of the loaf: if it comes out clean, it is done; if not, bake for a further 5–10 minutes.
6. Remove the loaf from the tin and leave to cool on a wire rack.

>> See steps on page 134

GINGERBREAD

Add the remaining ingredients to the refreshed starter and mix well.

Pour the mixture into a square baking tin.

Remove from the baking tin and cool on a wire rack.

CRANBERRY AND NUT LOAF

Choose your own favourite combination of nuts and fruit – all varieties taste great in this loaf.

INGREDIENTS

For the dough:
30 g wheat sourdough starter (page 71)
260 g white wheat or spelt flour, plus
    extra for dusting
95 g water
65 g milk
30 g honey (or agave)
5 g salt

For the filling:
45 g dry cranberries
40 g walnuts, chopped into small pieces

Filling variations:
hazelnut and raisin
almond and apricot
pecan and date

 TIP:
Dry roast nuts to enhance their flavour.
Allow them to cool down before you add
them to the dough.

METHOD

Day one

1. Measure the sourdough starter into a large bowl
   and return any remaining starter to the fridge.
2. Add 30 g flour and 30 g water. Stir and cover with
   cling film, and leave on the counter for around 8
   hours.

Day two

3. Add the remaining dough ingredients to the
   refreshed starter and knead well for 10 minutes.
   Put the dough in a bowl, cover with a shower cap
   and leave to rest for 4 hours.
4. Scrape the dough out on to a floury surface and
   scatter the fruit and nuts on the top. Gently knead
   them in.
5. Shape the dough into a tight ball and flour the top.
   Flour a 500 g round proving basket and gently place
   the dough in, floury side down. Cover the dough
   with a shower cap and leave to rise for 2 hours or
   until it passes the 'probe' test.
6. Preheat the oven to 230°C. Invert the basket to roll
   the dough gently onto a baking sheet lined with
   non-stick baking parchment. Put the dough in the
   oven and bake for 10 minutes. Reduce the heat to
   200°C and bake for a further 30 minutes.
7. Remove from the oven and leave to cool completely
   on a wire rack.

>> *See steps on page 138*

CRANBERRY AND NUT LOAF

Gently knead the fruit and nuts into the dough to avoid squashing the cranberries.

Flour the proving basket well.

Place the dough in the proving basket and cover with a shower cap.

Prove at room temperature for 2 hours and do the 'probe' test to check if the dough is ready for the oven.

AUSTRIAN CHRISTMAS BREAD

- -

Ground almonds, raisins and candied peel combine with anise to create a festive loaf that is delicious, and smells wonderful while baking.

INGREDIENTS

55 g wheat sourdough starter (page 71)
455 g white wheat or spelt flour
50 g ground almonds
55 g water
260 g milk
100 g sugar
8 g salt
1 tsp anise seeds
grated rind of 1 orange
100 g butter, at room temperature, cubed, plus extra melted butter for brushing

For the filling:
50 g raisins
50 g dried, mixed peel

METHOD

Day one

1. Measure the sourdough starter into a large bowl and return any remaining starter to the fridge.
2. Add 55 g flour and all the water. Stir and cover with cling film, and leave on the counter for around 8 hours.

Day two

3. Add the remaining dough ingredients, except the butter, to the refreshed starter and knead well for 10 minutes. Add the butter and knead for a further 10 minutes. Put the dough in a bowl, cover with a shower cap and leave to rest for 4 hours.
4. Scrape the dough out on to a floury surface and gently stretch it into a circle about 40 cm in diameter. Scatter the raisins and peel on the top. Take a side edge and fold it into the centre. Press down gently to cement the filling into the dough. Take the opposite side edge and fold it in to meet the first one. Press down gently. Now take a top edge and fold it into the centre of the dough, slightly overlapping the side folds. Finally take the bottom edge and fold it right over the dough to the opposite edge. Press down firmly with the heel of your hand to seal the seam, and place the dough, seam side down, on a baking sheet lined with non-stick baking parchment.
5. Cover the dough with a shower cap and leave to rest for 2 hours or until it passes the 'probe' test. Slash the top of the loaf in a diamond pattern and brush the top of the dough with the melted butter.
6. Preheat the oven to 200°C. Put the dough in the oven and bake for 45 minutes. Cover the dough with greaseproof paper or foil after 30 minutes so the fruit does not burn.
7. Remove from the oven and leave to cool completely on a wire rack.

Sweet Breads and Buns

>> *See steps on page 140*

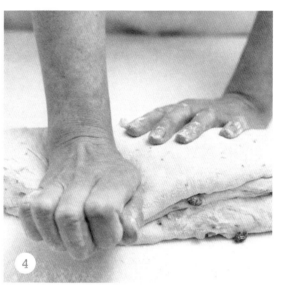

Scatter the raisins and peel over the dough and press down gently to cement the filling.

Cup your hand over the dough and use the heel of your hand to flatten and seal the edges.

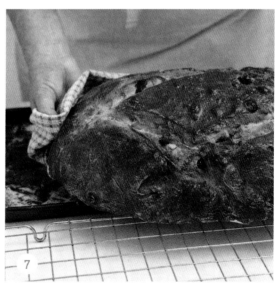

Slash the top of the loaf in a diamond pattern and glaze with melted butter.

Remove from the baking sheet and cool on a wire rack.

JASMINE TEA BUNS

- -

These deliciously light buns are the ideal afternoon tea treat. The subtle infusion of jasmine adds an aromatic twist.

INGREDIENTS

For the refreshed starter:
45 g white wheat flour
2 tbsp almond milk (unsweetened)
1 tbsp wheat sourdough starter (page 71)

For the dough:
1 tsp jasmine tea leaves
120 ml hot water (for steeping)
210 g white wheat flour
2 tbsp sugar
2 egg whites
½ tsp salt
2 tbsp unsalted butter

RECIPE BY YUKO IKEDA

Yuko was born and grew up in Japan but has since moved to the States and currently lives in Santa Monica. She worked her way up the restaurant ladder and is now pastry chef at Hinoki and the Bird in LA. Yuko is obsessed with baking and she blogs about baking and life in Santa Monica. www.akitchenblog.wordpress.com

METHOD

Day one

1. In a mixing bowl, combine the flour, almond milk and starter. Leave to prove at room temperature for 12 hours.

Day two

2. Steep the tea leaves in the hot water for 3 minutes. Drain the tea, reserving the leaves. Set aside 80 ml jasmine tea and chop and set aside 1 tbsp of the tea leaves.

3. Add the tea leaves and the remaining ingredients, except the salt and butter, to the refreshed starter, cover with oiled cling film and prove for 30 minutes.

4. Turn out onto a well floured surface, add the salt and knead until the gluten is developed (about 10 minutes).

5. Add the butter and knead the dough again until the gluten is very developed and you can see through the dough when stretched. Place the dough in a bowl, cover with oiled cling film and prove for 2½–4 hours.

6. Punch down the dough and put it in the fridge to prove overnight.

Day three

7. Remove the dough from the fridge and leave at room temperature for 1 hour.
8. Divide the dough into 4 pieces and pre-shape into rolls. Place on a floured baking sheet and set aside to rest for 30 minutes.
9. Shape the dough into buns and set aside for the final rise for 1–2 hours. Preheat the oven to 230°C.
10. Bake the buns for 25–30 minutes. Use a plant mister to spray inside the oven to create steam.
11. Remove from the oven and leave to cool completely on a wire rack.

Kneading tip

The key to soft crumbs and fluffy volume is strong development of the gluten's structure. Knead the dough until it becomes elastic and can be stretched very thinly but is still tough to break. If it's easy to poke and make a hole and the edge of the hole is rough, you need to knead the dough longer and keep checking the consistency of the dough.

CHOCOLATE SOURDOUGH CREAM CHEESE SWIRLS

- -

This breakfast bread is a true delight – soft and cakey with a hint of sweetness. There is just enough chocolate for a treat, but with a lightness that will get your day off to a great start.

INGREDIENTS

For the dough:
50 g wheat sourdough starter (page 71)
350 g white wheat flour, plus extra for
    dusting
50 g water
160 g milk
50 g sugar
50 g butter
1 egg
6 g salt
1½ tsp vanilla extract
30 g cocoa powder
1 tsp bicarbonate of soda
2 tbsp butter, melted and cooled to brush
    on the dough

For the filling:
225 g cream cheese, at room temperature
25 g sugar
½ tsp vanilla extract
1 egg
60 g unsalted butter
pinch of salt

For the icing (optional):
110 g icing sugar
1 tsp vanilla extract
60 g milk

METHOD

Day one

1. Measure the sourdough starter into a large bowl and return any remaining starter to the fridge.
2. Add 50 g flour and all the water. Stir and cover with cling film, and leave on the counter for around 8 hours.

Day two

3. Add the remaining dough ingredients to the refreshed starter and knead well for 10 minutes. Put the dough in a bowl, cover with a shower cap and leave for 4 hours. Meanwhile, using a hand beater, beat together the ingredients for the filling.
4. Scrape the dough onto a heavily floured surface and lightly flour the top. Roll it into a rectangle, around 55 x 25 cm. Gently spread the filling all over the dough – this is harder than it sounds so just be patient. Roll the dough up from one of the long ends, using a scraper to help you. Place it seam side down on the counter and slice the sausage of dough into 18 equal pieces.

5. Place the pieces of dough onto a well buttered baking sheet. Brush the tops and sides with butter and then cover with a shower cap and let the buns rest for 2 hours or until they pass the 'probe' test.

6. Preheat the oven to 180°C. Place the buns in the oven and bake for 30 minutes.

7. Remove the buns from the sheet with a spatula and leave them to cool completely on a wire rack.

8. If you would like to ice them, mix the icing ingredients together and then, with a spoon, dribble the icing all over the tops of the buns.

ADAPTED FROM A RECIPE BY JENNIFER WARD AND SHELLEY COONEY

Jenni and Shelley became friends while blogging, and they both fell in love with their sourdough starters. They had so much fun finding, developing and testing new ways to utilise their starters, that they soon found themselves trading recipes back and forth. They decided to start a website and monthly baking group dedicated to sharing their baking adventures with sourdough lovers around the world.
www.sourdoughsurprises.blogspot.com

TOP 10 SOURDOUGH TIPS

1. KEEP COOL

You will only kill the yeast if you add anything to the dough that is too hot. To avoid this happening, make sure the water or milk is at room temperature at most – cold is fine, hot is not. Additionally, if you dry-roast nuts, or sauté onions or other vegetables, let them cool completely before you add them to the dough.

2. KNEAD WELL

When working with wheat-family flour, your bread will be better if you knead it well. Whether by hand or machine, knead for a good ten minutes to activate the gluten, and use the windowpane test (page 151) to check for strength and stretchiness.

3. BUY GOOD-QUALITY FLOUR

Flour is the main event, so buy the best quality flour you can find: minimally processed, unbleached and, ideally, with no additives. This can be difficult and you will need to research mills, talk to millers and craft bakers, and experiment with different flours until you find those you like. It may be a little more expensive than big brand flour, but it is still relatively cheap. Flour does have a sell-by date, which should be respected, but it's usually pretty long so you can buy in bulk from a miller whose flour you like.

4. FEEL AND TASTE YOUR DOUGH

It is the relationship between how your dough feels and tastes, and how your bread feels and tastes that matters. Some people like salty bread, some like humid bread. Remember what your dough feels like and tastes like (a little raw dough won't hurt you), and then compare that to how the bread feels and tastes

when you eat it. Take notes, take photos and adjust as you become a more experienced baker.

5. BUY THERMOMETERS

So many problems can be avoided if your oven is at temperature. Beg, borrow or buy an oven thermometer and have your oven calibrated by an engineer if need be. Additionally, buy a digital probe thermometer so you can check the internal temperature of your bread – 98°C equals done.

6. ALLOW ENOUGH TIME FOR THE DOUGH TO RISE

The big drag when you are baking is when you have to go out or go to bed, and your dough is not ready for the oven. When you first start, leave plenty of time so you know your dough is ready. On a cold day, dough can take ages to rise and with a little experience you know when this is going to happen. You will also learn when you can pop your dough in the fridge to let it finish its rise while you are out (or sleeping). When you are first starting, give yourself a whole day just to be sure. A nice rainy day when going out seems too difficult and a good book seems just right. That is a perfect day to bake bread for the first time!

7. BE SELECTIVE WHEN YOU BUY EQUIPMENT

If you want to invest in a mixer, buy a good one rather than having to buy and replace mediocre machines. Invest in good tins that don't warp and that don't develop flaky sides and bases. That, however, is about it. Bowls, scrapers, spoons and measuring equipment do not need to be expensive.

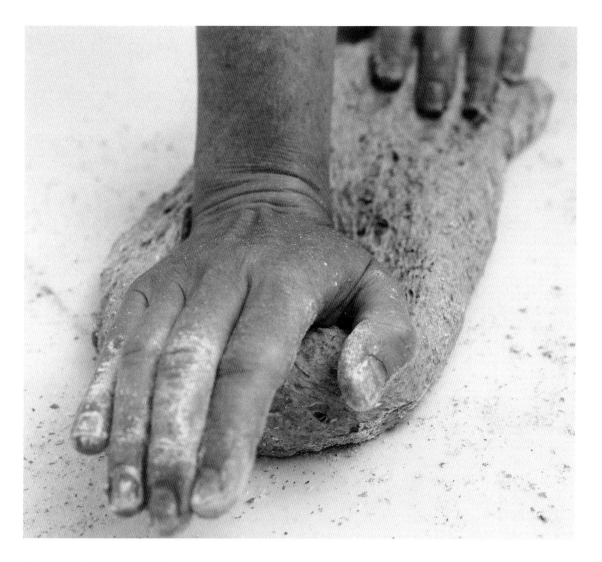

8. KEEP IT SIMPLE

When you are starting out, keep it simple. Simple bread is delicious – dubious combinations of flavours may not be so delicious.

9. HAVE A 'GO TO' BREAD

My 'go to' bread is 100 per cent rye. I will mix up enough dough for eight loaves (I have a big oven at home) and I will prove them in the fridge overnight. In the morning, I take them out, heat up the oven and pop them in. When they are cool, I freeze seven of them and take them out as I need them. The amount of work involved is maybe 30 minutes, and that includes washing up. Perfect!

10. RELAX

The only time the kitchen fairy deserts me is when I am angry or anxious. The thing to remember is the mantra: everything is good toasted, even if it's ugly. It's true.

BREAD AND HEALTH

Grains are basically grass seeds and humans don't eat grass. Eating grass or raw flour would give us an almighty tummy ache, as our tummies would struggle to know what to do and become bloated. Bread, and specifically bread made with wheat flour, has received a lot of bad press over the past few years, with articles about the dangers of consuming grains, and the rise of allergies and intolerances. If you do feel uncomfortable when you eat bread, you should get tested to see if you are a coeliac. Coeliacs must avoid any food with gluten, which includes bread made with wheat, rye, spelt, emmer, einkorn, kamut, barley and oats (unless they are labelled gluten free).

Some people who are not coeliacs still feel uncomfortable when they eat bread. There could be several reasons for this:

1. Overexposure: a daily diet of highly refined wheat-based breakfast cereal for breakfast, white bread sandwiches for lunch and pasta for dinner is limited in the extreme. Years of following that diet will put pressure on your system and could make you sensitive to wheat, or particularly, highly refined wheat. Eat everything in moderation is the advice our grannies gave us and they were probably right.

2. Changes in the wheat plant: since the widespread adoption of the combine harvester sometime between the world wars, wheat that is grown in the west has changed enormously. Not only does it look different, but its molecular structure and DNA are different. Scientists believe that certain people have difficulty digesting modern wheat, as it has changed so much and we haven't. Today, some farmers are returning to what is now called 'heritage wheat'. If you find you have a sensitivity to modern wheat, you could try heritage wheat as an alternative.

3. Flour: flour is not clearly labelled everywhere in the world. However, some countries do label flour and you may be surprised to learn that your average bag of flour may not just contain wheat, spelt or rye. It may, in fact, contain amylase, xylanase, ascorbic acid, niacin, reduced iron, thiamine, mononitrate, L-cysteine hydrochloride, azodicarbonamide or folic acid. In some countries, additives such as these are listed on the bag of flour. In other countries some of these additives are prohibited or included by law, and in still other countries the additives are not listed. If you are concerned, buy flour direct from a mill and ask what is in it.

4. Bread ingredients: the average loaf of bread shouldn't contain anything other than flour, water, salt and yeast. If your bread comes in a packet from the supermarket, the ingredients will be clearly displayed, but if your bread doesn't come in a packet, they won't necessarily be displayed. Additives in a plain loaf of white or brown bread may include some of those you read about in the section above on flour and, in addition, different kinds of sugar, fats, flour (the addition of soya flour, for example, is common), and additional gluten to help the dough stand up if it is made with weak wheat flour. Read the label if there is one, or talk to the baker if there isn't. And if there isn't a baker to talk to, you may want to reconsider buying the bread just in case.

GLOSSARY

Autolyse
This is the stage where the dough has a rest before being kneaded. It allows the gluten to develop before kneading takes place.

Baking stone
A flat, heatproof cooking platter that dough is placed on before being baked. They are available in different materials, including granite, iron, stone or ceramic.

Coeliac disease
A condition suffered by about 1 per cent of the population, for whom it is dangerous to eat gluten.

Elasticity
The ability of dough to 'bounce back'. Dough needs the right amount of elasticity to rise properly and keep hold of the gases inside.

Enriched bread
Enriched dough contains eggs, butter and/or milk, and usually sugar too. Added ingredients will have an impact on the amount of time the dough takes to rise: certain ingredients slow down the yeast and others weigh down the dough.

Fermenting/proofing/rising
These are different terms for the step in the baking process when the dough is being filled with carbon dioxide to become lighter, to develop flavour, and to become more digestible. Some recipes call for more than one rise, so the dough can achieve a really light texture and a beautiful shape.

Final dough
The dough that you will shape and let rise before putting it in the oven to bake.

Gluten
This is a protein created when glutenin and gliadin form a bond. When you knead bread you 'activate' the gluten and create a membrane that traps carbon dioxide bubbles as they form, giving volume to the bread. Gluten also gives bread its chewy texture.

Hydration
This is a baking term that refers to how much water is in a dough as a percentage of the flour. Sixty per cent hydration, for example, is a dough in which the amount of water is 60 per cent of the amount of flour.

Lame

A special razor used to make cuts in dough before it goes in the oven, both to control cracking and to make an attractive pattern.

Levain/poolish/sponge

These are names used for sourdough starters that you are bound to come across if you get the sourdough baking bug.

Peel

A long-handled paddle that is used to place and remove bread from a baking stone or the bottom of a bread oven.

Pre-dough

Some recipes involve several steps. A pre-dough contains the refreshed starter and some of the ingredients for the final dough. You create a pre-dough to build flavour, help dough rise, and develop a chewier texture in the bread.

Proofing basket (banneton)

Basket made of cane or pressed wood (or even plastic) in which dough rises for a more rustic and traditional look.

Punch down/de-gas/knock back

Recipes sometimes ask you to 'punch down' or 'de-gas' the dough after the first rise. This serves many purposes: it expels old carbon dioxide gases, making room for more; it moves the dough around at a microscopic level, giving the yeast new food to eat, it strengthens the dough, once it is shaped, enabling it to rise more easily

Refreshed starter

The bubbly, sweet-smelling result of adding fresh flour and water to your sourdough starter. You add the remaining dough ingredients to your refreshed starter to make bread.

Scraper

A small, thin, rectangular plastic paddle with no handle that is invaluable for cutting, kneading and moving dough.

Sourdough starter

This is the basic paste of flour and water in which the natural yeast is trapped. It takes 4 to 5 days to make and involves gradually adding flour and water together. Keep it in the fridge in an airtight container, when it has 'taken', and take it out when you need to use it.

Spelt, Emmer, Einkorn, Kamut

Varieties of flour that are milled from grains that are distant cousins of wheat. They all contain gluten but have different characteristics to wheat, so the dough and the bread will have a different texture and flavour.

Windowpane test

Once you have kneaded your dough, cut off a small piece and gently stretch it under a light (sunlight or electric). You should be able to stretch it so thinly that you can see light through it. If it tears before you get to that stage, knead it for 2 to 3 minutes more and try again. This technique is easy to do with all white wheat, harder to do with whole grain flour and impossible with rye

RESOURCES

AMAZON

Whichever country you live in, Amazon is an excellent source of baking equipment and ingredients. From tins to proving baskets, from flour to dried fruit, you can buy almost anything you need to bake sourdough bread from this website.
www.amazon.com

KITCHENAID AND KENWOOD

These are both excellent brands of freestanding mixers with dough hooks. Look on their websites for their latest information and prices.
www.kitchenaid.com
www.kenwood.com

BROTFORMEN

This is the best place to find all manner of proving baskets and other containers for rising bread. The company is based in Germany but will ship orders across the EU and to the USA and Canada.
www.brotformen24.de

SOURCING EQUIPMENT

If you type 'bakery supplies online' into your internet search engine you will find a great deal of options.

SOURCING FLOUR

If you type 'stone-milled flour online' into your internet search engine you will find excellent providers of good-quality, stone-milled, organic and non-organic flour. Shipping flour is not cheap but if you buy it in bulk you will find it is no more expensive than going to the supermarket and carrying it home in small bags.

INDEX

ACKNOWLEDGEMENTS

For Harriet, who gave me my first sourdough starter and cook book. For all my students, who continue to encourage and challenge me. To Jo Turner, who gave this book a second chance. To Lucy Heeley, for being inventive, flexible and practical in her approach to the food prep and styling. Quintet Publishing would also like to thank Andrew James Worldwide for kindly supplying kitchen equipment for the photoshoot.

ABOUT THE AUTHORS

Jane Mason founded Virtuous Bread (www.virtuousbread.com) in 2010 to make it fun and easy for people all over the world to make, find and learn about bread, and in so doing to forge the link between bread and virtue. Jane bakes, teaches baking and speaks about bread as a catalyst for social change. Jane has had the fortune to bake with excellent bakers from South Africa to Sweden, and all points in between, and it is this knowledge of global bread and its role in the lives of billions of people all over the world that makes her special. She is the author of *All You Knead Is Bread* and *The Book of Buns*.

Ed Wood is a sourdough enthusiast and owner of Ed Wood's International Sourdough (www.sourdo.com). The company prides itself on being a source of authentic sourdough cultures, and ships to countries all over the world. He is the author of *Classic Sourdoughs: A Home Baker's Handbook*.

PICTURE CREDITS